AF333981

FACE ANALYSIS, MODELING AND RECOGNITION SYSTEMS

Edited by **Tudor Barbu**

INTECHOPEN.COM

Face Analysis, Modeling and Recognition Systems
Edited by Tudor Barbu

Published by InTech

Janeza Trdine 9, 51000 Rijeka, Croatia

Edition 2014

Publishing Process Manager Mirna Cvijic

Technical Editor Teodora Smiljanic

Cover Designer InTech Design Team

Image Copyright marema, 2011. Used under license from Shutterstock.com

Additional hard copies can be obtained from orders@intechopen.com

Face Analysis, Modeling and Recognition Systems, Edited by Tudor Barbu
p. cm.
ISBN 978-953-307-738-3

Contents

Preface

Face recognition represents an important computer vision domain that has been vividly researched in the last decades. Face recognition is a task that the human vision system performs almost effortlessly and successfully, but artificial face recognition represents still a difficult task.

The history of the automatic facial recognition area begins in 1960s, but this technology has been propelled into the spotlight by the major advancements in computing capability and research initiatives of the past 20 years. In spite of more than two decades of extensive research, numerous papers being published in prestigious journals and conference volumes in that period, the development of a computer-based artificial facial recognition system having capabilities comparable with those of human vision systems represents an unachieved goal.

Artificial face recognition is quite difficult because of many factors, such as viewpoint, lightning conditions, facial expressions, aging effects and occlusions. While humans can recognize easily faces affected by these factors, the computer systems are not even close to this.

Face recognition represents both a pattern recognition and biometric domain. As any biometric system, a facial recognition system performs two major operations: person identification and verification. Face identification represents a supervised pattern recognition process performing two other operations: feature extraction and classification respectively. Also, face recognition represents the most popular and the most successful object recognition area.

Human face is a physiological biometric identifier widely used in biometric authentication. Face recognition is preferable to many other biometric technologies because of its non-intrusive character and because it is very easy to use. The main application areas of facial recognition are access control, surveillance systems, robotics, human-computer interactions and medical diagnosis.

The purpose of this book, entitled *Face Analysis, Modeling and Recognition Systems* is to provide a concise and comprehensive coverage of artificial face recognition domain across four major areas of interest: biometrics, robotics, image databases and cognitive models. Our book aims to provide the reader with current state-of-the-art in these domains.

The book is composed of 12 chapters which are grouped in four sections. The chapters in this book describe numerous novel face analysis techniques and approach many unsolved issues. The first section, entitled *Face Recognition Systems using Principal Component Analysis*, consists of the first two chapters and deals with the PCA or Eigenfaces approach, which represents a benchmark face recognition technique. While Chapter 1 describes an improved Eigenface-based recognition system applied successfully in the robotics field, in Chapter 2 are presented two novel face recognition methods. A PCA-based recognition approach is compared with a robust face authentication technique using a set of 2D Gabor filters for facial feature extraction.

The second book section, *Feature-based Face Detection, Analysis and Recognition Algorithms*, is composed of the next four chapters. Numerous innovative face detection, processing, analysis and recognition algorithms are proposed in this section.

Chapter 3 investigates various frequency domain facial feature extraction techniques based on discrete transforms, emphasizing their advantages: compact extraction of the face information, easy implementation, robustness against condition changes and fast processing. Chapter 4 analyzes the task of developing an automatic face recognition system using local feature-based methods. Three local feature based algorithms are implemented for AFR. They use Harris corner detectors for feature point detection and NN- classifiers.

In Chapter 5 the authors introduce two methods for evaluation of the facial paralysis degree for clinical purpose. They propose a simple and efficient scheme for grading facial paralysis based on corner and salient point detection. Chapter 6 explores face recognition, classification, inversion within the framework of the multidimensional space model. The successfully experiments described in this chapter prove that the MDS model enhances our understanding of face recognition.

The third section, entitled *Facial Image Database Development - Recognition Evaluation and Security Algorithms*, contains the next two chapters of the book. Development of face image databases is important because these databases are essential to evaluate the face recognition procedures. Chapter 7 presents a face database created for investigating the effect of out-of-focus blur on the performances of face detection and recognition systems. In Chapter 8 the author considers improving the security of facial image databases by using a fragile digital watermarking technique.

The last section, entitled *Cognitive Models for Face Recognition Disorders*, is composed of the last four chapters of this book. In this section there are investigated the most popular facial recognition medical disorders. Chapter 9 analyzes the roles of featural and configurational processing in face recognition performed by humans. The authors examine patients suffering of diseases producing aberrant face recognition, like prosopagnosia and schizophrenia, to determine how featural and configurational information contribute to human face recognition.

The psychiatric disorders of face recognition are also investigated in Chapter 10. The chapter represents a literature survey of face misidentification syndromes and neurocognitive models for face recognition. In Chapter 11 the issue of face recognition heritability is investigated. Its authors try to demonstrate that face recognition represents an inherited cognitive ability by studying the hereditary prosopagnosia. Chapter 12, the final chapter of the book, first presents an overview of the recent research on the neural mechanisms of facial recognition. Then, the authors review the neuropsychological findings of behavioral, structural and functional studies on abnormalities of face recognition in patients with schizophrenia disease.

The authors who contributed to this book work as professors and researchers at important institutions across the globe, and are recognized experts in the scientific fields approached here. The topics in this book cover a wide range of issues related to face analysis and here are offered many solutions to open issues. We anticipate that this book will be of special interest to researchers and academics interested in computer vision, biometrics, image processing, pattern recognition and medical diagnosis.

Tudor Barbu, PhD
Institute of Computer Science,
Romanian Academy, Iaşi branch
Romania

Part 1

Face Recognition Systems Using Principal Component Analysis

1

An Improved Face Recognition System for Service Robot Using Stereo Vision

Widodo Budiharto[1], Ari Santoso[2], Djoko Purwanto[2] and Achmad Jazidie[2]
[1]Dept. of Informatics Engineering, BINUS University, Jakarta
[2]Dept. of Electrical Engineering, Institute of Technology Sepuluh Nopember, Surabaya
Indonesia

1. Introduction

Service robot is an emerging technology in robot vision, and demand from household and industry will be increased significantly in the future. General vision-based service robot should recognizes people and obstacles in dynamic environment and accomplishes a specific task given by a user. The ability to face recognition and natural interaction with a user are the important factors for developing service robots. Since tracking of a human face and face recognition are an essential function for a service robot, many researcher have developed face-tracking mechanism for the robot (Yang M., 2002) and face recognition system for service robot(Budiharto, W., 2010).

The objective of this chapter is to propose an improved face recognition system using PCA(Principal Component Analysis) and implemented to a service robot in dynamic environment using stereo vision. The variation in illumination is one of the main challenging problem for face recognition. It has been proven that in face recognition, differences caused by illumination variations are more significant than differences between individuals (Adini et al., 1997). Recognizing face reliably across changes in pose and illumination using PCA has proved to be a much harder problem because eigenfaces method comparing the intensity of the pixel. To solve this problem, we have improved the training images by generate random value for varying the intensity of the face images.

We proposed an architecture of service robot and database for face recognition system. A navigation system for this service robot and depth estimation using stereo vision for measuring distance of moving obstacles are introduced. The obstacle avoidance problem is formulated using decision theory, prior and posterior distribution and loss function to determine an optimal response based on inaccurate sensor data. Based on experiments, by using 3 images per person with 3 poses (frontal, left and right) and giving training images with varying illumination, it improves the success rate for recognition. Our proposed method very fast and successfully implemented to service robot called Srikandi III in our laboratory.

This chapter is organized as follows. Improved method and a framework for face recognition system is introduced in section 2. In section 3, the system for face detection and depth estimation for distance measurement of moving obstacles are introduced. Section 4, a detailed implementation of improved face recognition for service robot using stereo vision is presented. Finally, discussions and future work are drawn in section 5.

2. Improved face recognition system using PCA

The face is our primary focus of attention in developing a vision based service robot to serves peoples. Unfortunatelly, developing a computational model of face recognition is quite difficult, because faces are complex, meaningful visual stimuli and multidimensional. Modelling of face images can be based on statistical model such as Principal Component Analysis (PCA) (Turk & Pentland, 1991) and Linear Discriminat analysis (LDA) (Etemad & Chellappa, 1997; Belhumeur et.al, 1997), and physical modelling based on the assumption of certain surface reflectance properties, such as Lambertian surface (Zoue et al., 2007). Linear Discriminant Analysis (LDA) is a method of finding such a linear combination of variables which best separates two or more classes. Constrasting ther PCA which encodes information in an orthogonal linear space, the LDA which also known as fischerfaces method encodes discriminatory information in a linear separable space of which bases are not necessary orthogonal. However, the LDA result is mostly used as part of a linear classifier (Zhao et al., 1998).

PCA is a standard statistical method for feature extraction by reduces the dimension of input data by a linear projection that maximizes the scatter of all projected samples. The scheme is based on an information theory approach that decomposes faces images into a small set of characteristic feature images called eigenfaces, as the principal components of the initial training set of face images. Recognition is performed by projecting a new image into the subspace spanned by the eigenfaces called face space, and then classifying the face by comparing its position in face space with the positions of known individuals. PCA based approaches typically include two phases: training and classification. In the training phase, an eignespace is established from the training samples using PCA and the training face images are mapped to the eigenspace for classification. In the classification phase, an input face is projected to the same eignespace and classified by an appropriate classifier (Turk & Pentland, 1991). Let a face image $I(x, y)$ be a two-dimensional N by N array of (8-bit) intensity values. An image may also be considered as a vector of dimension N^2, so that a typical image of size 256 by 256 becomes a vector of dimension 65,536 (a point in 65,536-dimensional space). If Φ is face images and M training set face images, we can compute the eigenspace u_i :

$$u_i = \sum_{k=1}^{M} v_{ik}\Phi_k \quad i = 1, 2, \dots, M \tag{1}$$

Where u_i and v_{ik} are the ith eigenspace and the kth value of the ith eigenvector. Then, we can determining which face class provides the best description of an input face images to find the face class k by using the euclidian distance ε_k between the new face projection Ω, the class projection Ω_k and threshold θ using formula :

$$\varepsilon_k = \|\Omega - \Omega_k\| < \theta \tag{2}$$

The stereo camera used in this research is 640x480 pixels. The size of face image is cropped to 92x112pixels using Region of Interest method (ROI) as shown in figure below. These images also used as training images for face recognition system. We use histogram equalization for contrast adjustment using the image's histogram. This method usually increases the global contrast of many images, especially when the usable data of the image is represented by close contrast values. Through this adjustment, the intensities can be better distributed on the histogram. This allows for areas of lower local contrast to gain a higher contrast. Histogram equalization accomplishes this by effectively spreading out the most frequent intensity values.

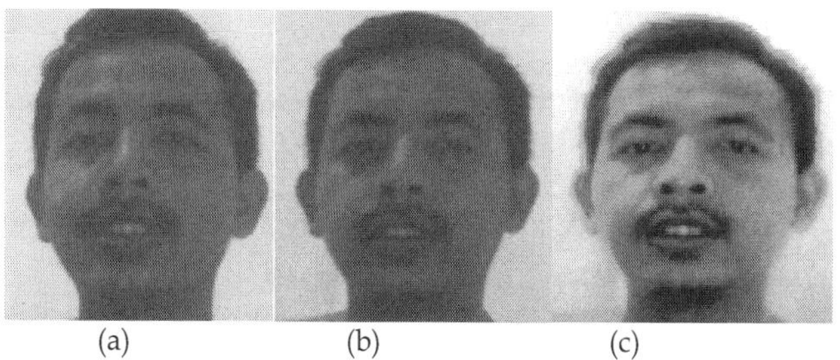

(a)   (b)   (c)

Fig. 1. Original image (a) , then applied preprocessing image to greyscale image (b) and histogram equalization (c).

The illumination variation is one of the main challenging problems that a practical face recognition system needs to deal with. Various methods have been proposed to solve the problem, named as face and illumination modeling, illumination invariant feature extraction and preprocessing and normalization. In (Belhumeur & Kriegman 1998), an illumination model illumination cone is proposed for the first time. The authors proved that the set of n-pixel images of a convex object with a Lambertian reflectance function, under an arbitrary number of point light sources at infinity, formed a convex polyhedral cone in IR^n named as illumination cone (Belhumeur & Kriegman 1998). In this research, we construct images under different illumination conditions by generate a random value for brightness level developed using Visual C++ technical Pack using this formula :

$$I_o(x,y) = I_i(x,y) + c \tag{3}$$

Where I_o is the intensity value after brightness operation applied, I_i is the intensity value before brightness operation and c is a brightness level. The effect of brightness level shown at histogram below:

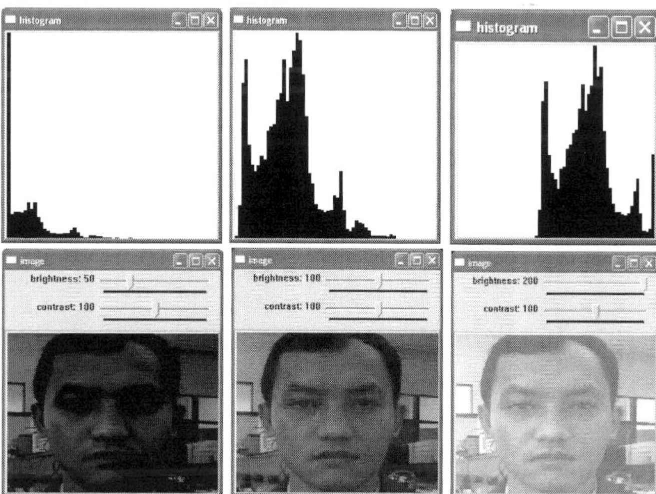

Fig. 2. Effect of varying the illumination for a face.

We have developed a Framework of Face recognition system for vision-based service robot. This framework very usefull as a information for robot to identify a customer and what items ordered by a customer. First, to storing training faces of customers, we have proposed a database for face recognition that consists of a table faces, products and order. An application interface for this database shown below :

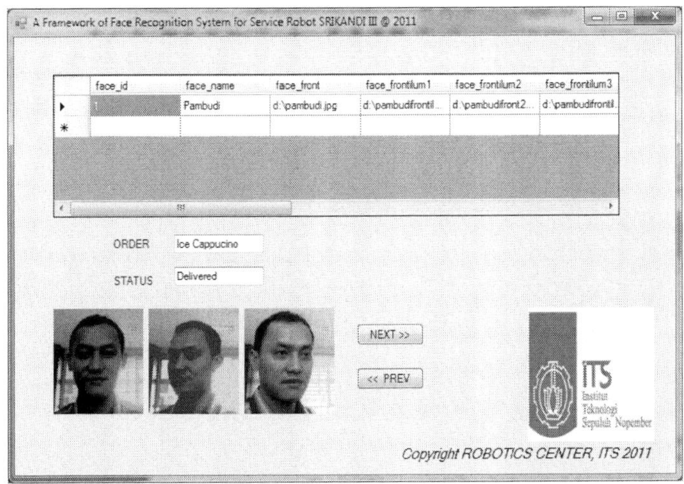

Fig. 3. We have proposed face databases using 1 table, 3 images used for each person (frontal, left and right poses).

We have identified the effect varying illumination to the accuracy of recognition for our database called ITS face database as shown in table 1 :

Training images	Testing images	Success rate
No varying illumination		
6	6	100%
12	6	100%
24	6	100%
Varying Illumination		
6	6	50.00%
12	6	66.00%
24	6	100%
24	10	91.60%

Table 1. Testing images without and with varying illumination. Results shows that by giving enough training images with variation of illumination generated randomly, the success rate of face recognition will be improved.

We also evaluate the result of our proposed face recognition system and compared with ATT and Indian face database using Face Recognition Evaluator developed by Matlab. Each of face database consists of 10 sets of people's face. Each set of ITS face database consists of 3 poses (front, left, right) and varied with illumination. ATT face database consists of 9 differential facial expression and small occlusion (by glass) without variation of illumination . The Indian face database consists of eleven pose orientation without variation of illumination and the size of each image is too small than ITS and ATT face database. The success rate comparison between 3 face databases shown below:

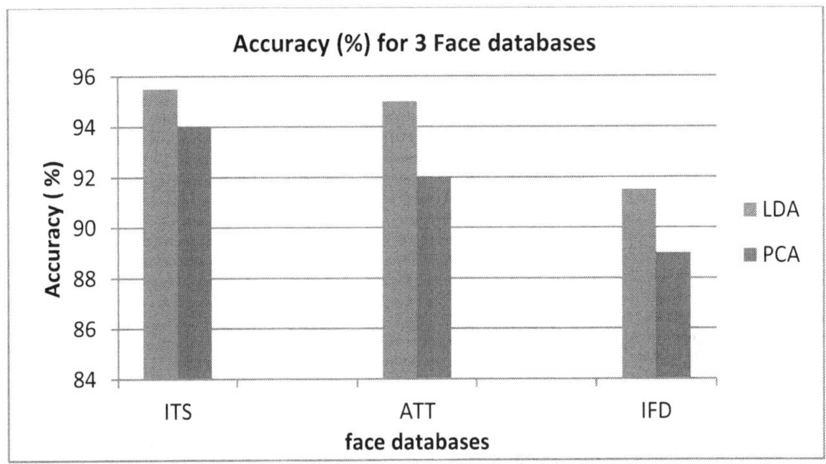

Fig. 4. Success rate comparison of face recognition between 3 faces databases, each using 10 sets face. It shown clearly that ITS database have highest success rate than ATT and Indian face database when the illumination of testing images is varied. The success rate using PCA in our proposed method and ITS face database is 95.5 %, higher than ATT face database 95.4%.

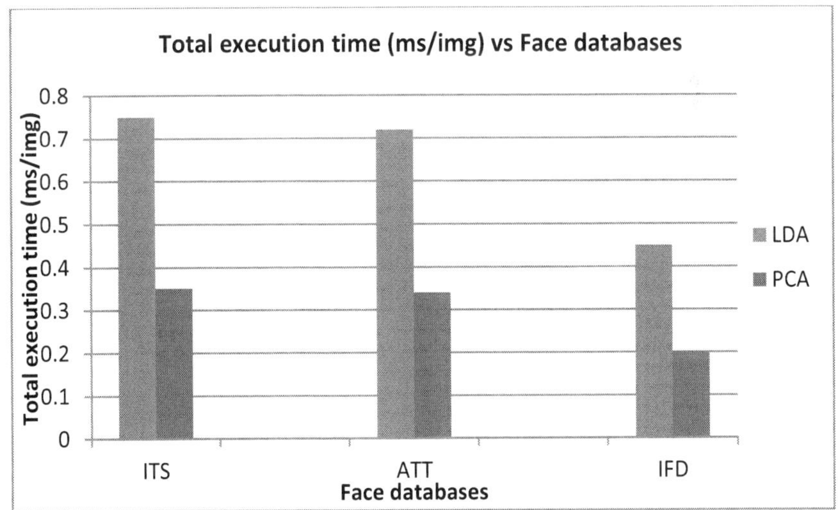

Fig. 5. For total execution time, we can see the Indian face database (IFD) is shortest because the size of each image is lowest then ITS and ATT.

3. Face detection and depth estimation using stereo vision

We have developed a system for face detection using Haar cascade classifier and depth estimation for measuring distance of peoples as moving obstacles using stereo vision. The camera used is a Minoru 3D stereo camera. The reason for using stereo camera in order robot able to estimate distance to obstacle without additional sensor(only 1 ultrasonic sensor infront of robot for emergency), so the cost for development can be reduced. Let's start froma basic conce where a point q captured by camera, the point in the front image frame $^Ip(^Ip_x,{}^Ip_y)$ is the projection of the point in camera frame $^Cp(^Cp_x,{}^Cp_y,{}^Cp_z)$ onto the front image frame. Here, f denotes the focal length of the lens. Fig. 6 shown is the projection of a point on the front image frame.

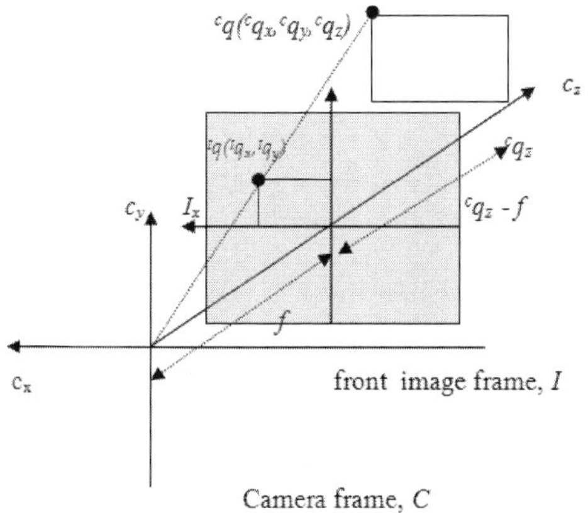

Fig. 6. Projection of point on front image frame.

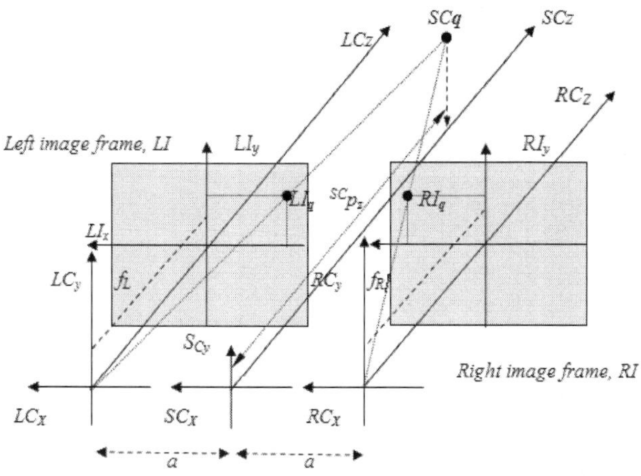

Fig. 7. Stereo Imaging model

In the stereo imaging model, the tree-dimensional points in stereo camera frame are projected in the left and the right image frame. On the contrary, using the projection of the points onto the left and right image frame, the three-dimensional points positions in stereo camera frame can be located. Fig. 7 shows the stereo imaging model using the left front image frame *LF* and right front image frame *RF* (Purwanto, D., 2001).

By using stereo vision, we can obtain the position of each moving obstacle in the images, then we can calculate and estimate the distance of the moving obstacle. The three-dimensional point in stereo camera frame can be reconstructed using the two-dimensional projection of point in left front image frame and in right front image frame using formula:

$$
{}^{SC}\mathbf{q} = \begin{bmatrix} {}^{SC}q_x \\ {}^{SC}q_y \\ {}^{SC}q_z \end{bmatrix} = \frac{2}{{}^{RI}q_x - {}^{LI}q_x} \begin{bmatrix} \frac{1}{2}a\left({}^{RI}q_x + {}^{LI}q_x\right) \\ a\,{}^{RI}q_y \\ f\,a \end{bmatrix} \tag{4}
$$

$$
\text{Note that } {}^{LI}q_y = {}^{RI}q_y
$$

Figure shown below is the result of 2 moving obstacle identification using stereo vision, distance of obstacle obtained using depth estimation based on eq. 4. State estimation is used for handling inaccurate vision sensor, we adopted it using Bayesian approach for probability of obstacle denoted as *p(Obstacle)* and probability of direction *p(Direction)* with the *value* between 0-1.

Fig. 8. Robot succesfully identified and estimated distance of 2 moving obstacles in front of robot.

4. Implementation to vision-based service robot

4.1 Architecture of service robot

We have developed a vision-based service robot called Srikandi III with the ability to face recognition and avoid people as moving obstacles, this wheeled robot is next generation from Srikandi II (Budiharto, W. 2010). A mobile robot involving two actuator wheels is considered as a system subject to nonholonomic constraints. Consider an autonomous wheeled mobile robot and position in the Cartesian frame of coordinates shown in fig. 10, where x_R and y_R are the two coordinates of the origin **P** of the moving frame and θ_R is the robot orientation angle with respect to the positive x-axis. The rotation angle of the right and left wheel denoted as φ_r and φ_l and radius of the wheel by R thus the configuration of the mobile robot c_R can be described by five generalized coordinates such as :

$$c_R = \left(x_R, y_R, \theta_R, \varphi_r, \varphi_l\right)^T \tag{5}$$

Based on fig, 10, v_R is the linear velocity, ω_R is the angular velocity, r_R and λ_R are radial and angular coordinate of the robot (Mahesian, 2007). The kinematics equations of motion for the robot given by :

$$\dot{x}_R = v_R \cos\theta_R \tag{6}$$

$$\dot{y}_R = v_R \sin\theta_R \tag{7}$$

$$\dot{\theta}_R = \omega_R \tag{8}$$

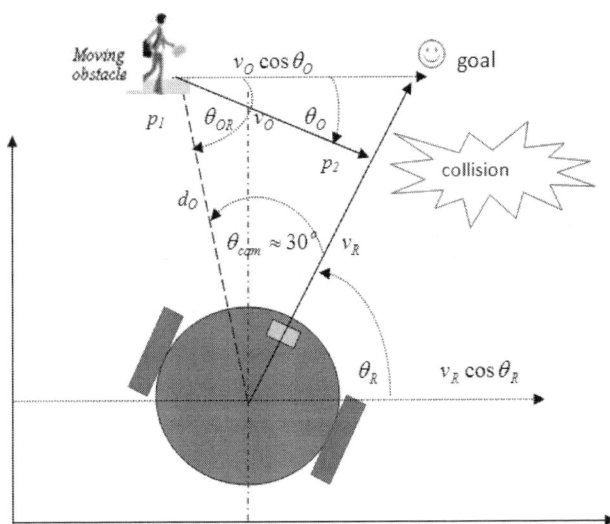

Fig. 9. Proposed Cartesian model of mobile robot with moving obstacle

The angular velocity of the right and left wheel can be obtained by :

$$\omega_r = \frac{d\varphi_r}{dt} \text{ and } \omega_l = \frac{d\varphi_l}{dt} \tag{9}$$

Finally, the linear velocity v_R can be formulated as :

$$v_R = R(\omega_r + \omega_l) / 2 \tag{10}$$

Camera become important sensor if we want to identify specific object such as face, small object, shape etc) that could not identified by other sensor such as ultrasonic sensors. Camera as a vision sensor have limitation in angle area for capturing object. We defined θ_{cam} as a maximum angle that moving obstacle can be detected by camera used in this research. Based on the fig. 1, we defined angle between moving obstacle and robot θ_{OR} as:

$$\theta_{OR} = 180° - (\theta_R + \theta_{cam}) \tag{11}$$

$\theta_O, \theta_{OR}, \theta_{Cam}, \theta_R, v_R$ and v_O are very important properties for calculating whether robot will collides or not with moving obstacle. To calculate the speed of moving obstacle v_O based on vision is a complex task, we propose the model for calculate the v_O that moving with angle θ_O detected by the camera, whereas at the same time the robot moving with speed v_R to the goal with angle θ_R, we need 2 point of tracked images with interval $t = 1$ second, then the difference of pixel position obtained.

Based on the fig. 10, the equation for estimates v_O when moving obstacle and robot are moving is :

$$v_O \cos\theta_O = \frac{|p_2 - p_1|s}{t} + v_R \cos\theta_R \tag{12}$$

Finally, we can simplified the eq. 12 as :

$$v_O = \frac{|p_2 - p_1|s}{t \cos\theta_O} + \frac{v_R \cos\theta_R}{\cos\theta_O} \tag{13}$$

Where p_1 and p_2 are the position of the obstacle in pixel and s is the scaling factor in cm/pixel. We proposed mechanism for predicting collision using time t needed for robot to collides the moving obstacle that move with orientation θ_O as shown in fig, 1 and should be greater than threshold T for robot to allowing moving forward, can be calculated by formula:

$$t = \frac{d_O \sin\theta_{OR}}{(v_R \sin\theta_R + v_O \sin\theta_O)} \tag{14}$$

Note: if $t <= T$ then robot stop

if $t > T$ then robot moving forward

Fig. 10 shown below is an architecture of service robot Srikandi III that utilizing stereo camera, compass and distance sensors. Because this robot need to recognizes and tracks people, many supporting functions developed and integrated such as face recognition system, static and moving obstacles detection and moving obstacle tracking, to make the robot robust and reliable. We developed efficient Faces database used by face recognition system for recognizing customer. There is interface program between Laptop for coordinating robot controller. 1 controller using Propeller used for coordinating actuator and communication with the and used for distance measurement. Srikandi III implements path planning based on the free area obtained from the landmark by edge and smoothing operation.

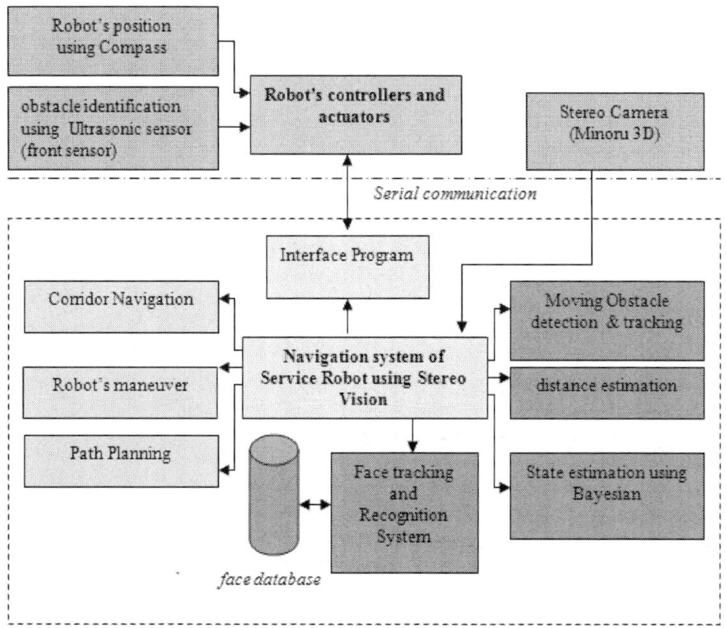

Fig. 10. General architecture of service robot called Srikandi III. Hardware and software parts are separated by the dashed line. All arrows indicate dataflow.

Because of the limitation of stereo camera used for distance measurement, Kalman filtering applied to make sure the measurement of distance between robot and obstacle more stable. The prototype of service Robot Srikandi III that utilized a low cost stereo camera using Minoru 3D is shown in fig. 11:

4.2 Proposed navigation system of vision-based service robot
4.2.1 Flow chart of a navigation system
The service robot should navigates from start to goal position and go back to home savely. We assumed the when robot running, people as moving obstacle may collides with the robot. So we proposed a method for obstacles avoidance for Service robot in general as shown in Fig. 12. The model of experiment for customer identification is using stereo camera, the advantage is we can estimate the distance of customer/obstacles and direction's movement of obstacles. There is no map or line tracking to direct a robot to an identified customer. Image captured by stereo camera used as testing images to be processed by Haar classifier to detect how many people in the images, and face recognition by PCA. We

Fig. 11. Prototype of Service robot Srikandi III using stereo camera

implementing visual tracking to heading a robot to a customer. Robot continuously measures the distance of obstacle and send the data to Laptop. The next step is multiple moving obstacle detection and tracking. If there is no moving obstacle, robot run from start to goal position in normal speed. If moving obstacle appeared and collision will occurred, robot will maneuver to avoids obstacle.

Figure shown below is a flowchart that describes general mechanism for our method for detecting multiple moving obstacle and maneuver to avoids collision with the obstacles.

To implement the flowchart above for service robot that should recognize the customer and have the ability for multiple moving obstacle avoidance, we have developed algorithm and programs consist of 3 main modules such as a framework for face recognition system, multiple moving obstacle detection and Kalman filtering as state estimator for distance measurement using stereo camera.

4.2.2 Probabilistic robotics for navigation system

Camera as vision sensor sometimes have distortion, so Bayesian decision theory used to state estimation and determine the optimal response for the robot based on inaccurate sensor data. Bayesian decision rule probabilistically estimate a dynamic system state from noisy observations. Examples of measurement data include camera images and range scan. If x is a quantity that we would like to infer from y, the probability $p(x)$ will be referred to as prior probability distribution. The Bayesian update formula is applied to determine the new posterior $p(x, y)$ whenever a new observation is obtained:

$$p(x, y) = \frac{p(y|x,z)p(x|z)}{p(y|z)} \qquad (15)$$

To apply Bayesian decision theory for obstacle avoidance, we consider the appearance of an unexpected obstacle to be a random event, and optimal solution for avoiding obstacles is obtained by trading between maneuver and stop action. If we want service robot should stay on the path in any case, strategies to avoid moving obstacle include:

- Maneuver, if service robot will collides.
- stop, if moving obstacle too close to robot.

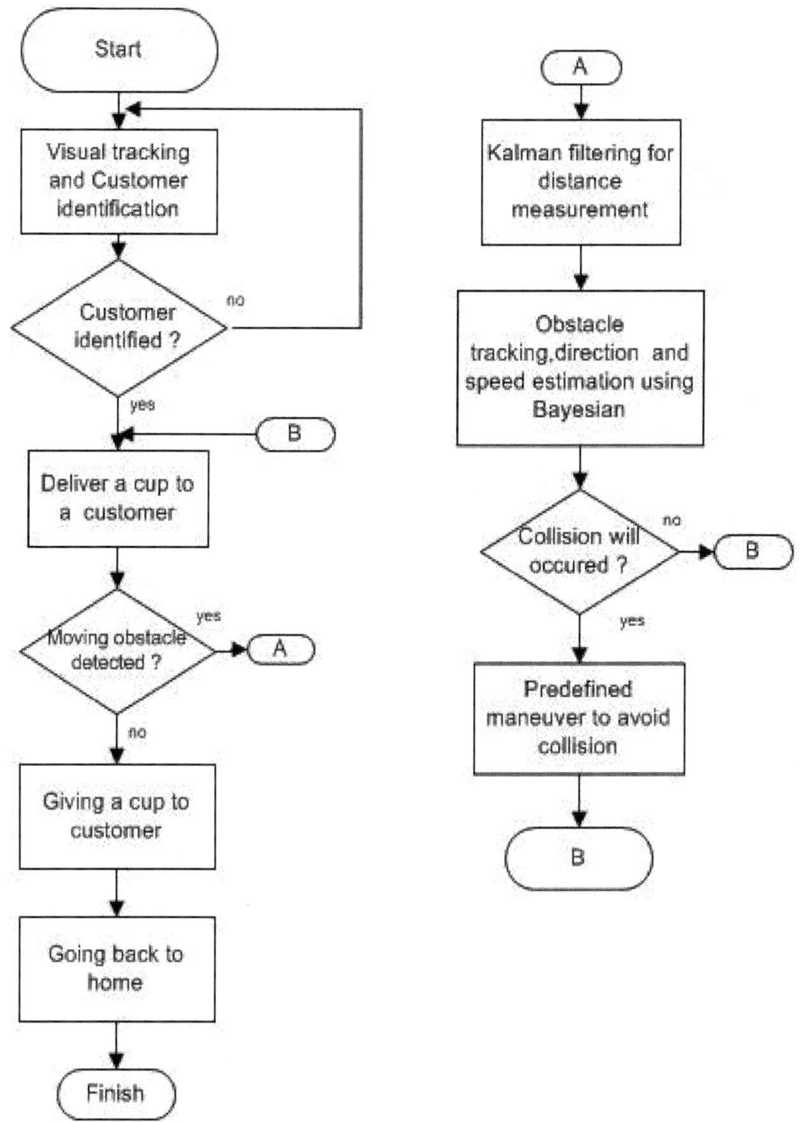

Fig. 12. Flow chart of Navigation System from start to goal position for service robot.

Then, we restrict the action space denoted as **A** as :

$$A = \left(a_{1,}a_{2},a_{3}\right) \tag{16}$$

$$= \text{maneuver to left, maneuver to right, stop} \tag{17}$$

We define a loss function $L(a, \theta)$ which gives a measure of the loss incurred in taking action a when the state is θ. The robot should chooses an action a from the set **A** of possible actions based on the observation **z** of the current state of the path θ. This gives the posterior distribution of θ as:

$$p(\theta \mid z) = \frac{p(z \mid \theta)p(\theta)}{\sum p(z \mid \theta)p(\theta)} \tag{18}$$

Then, based on the posterior distribution in (17), we can compute the posterior expected loss of an action (Hu, H et al., 1994):

$$B(p(\theta \mid z),a) = \sum_{\theta} L(\theta,a)p(\theta \mid z) \tag{19}$$

The figure below shows the proposed model of maneuvering on the service robot, pL which is the probability of moving obstacle leads to the left, and pR the probability of moving obstacle leads to the right. By estimating the direction of motion of the obstacle, then the most appropriate action to avoid to the right / left side can be determined, to minimize collisions with these obstacles. If there are more than 1 moving obstacle, then robot should identified the nearest moving obstacle to avoid it, and the direction of maneuver should be opposite with the direction of moving obstacle.

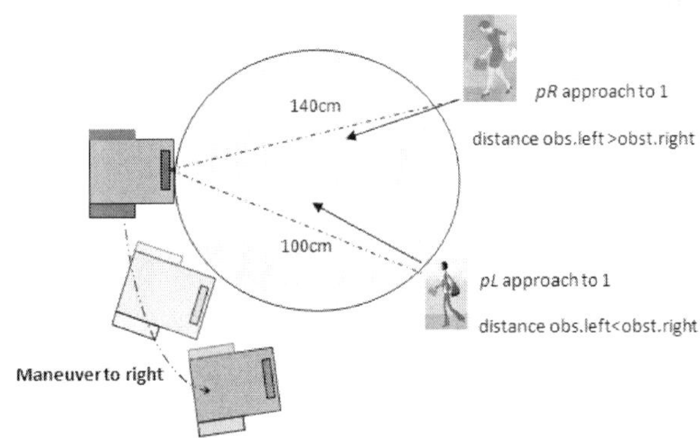

(a)

Moreover, $\varphi_j \in (H^1(\Omega))^3$, $\forall j$. Let us associate with Q the $[3M \times 3M]$ matrix $\tilde{Q} = A^T A$, where $A : R^{3M} \to (L^2(\Omega))^3$ is given by $AY = \left[\sum_{i=1}^{M} \Phi_i y_1^i, \sum_{i=1}^{M} W_i^1 y_2^i, \sum_{i=1}^{M} W_i^1 y_3^i \right]$, $Y = \{y_1^i, y_2^i, y_3^i\}_{i=1}^{M}$, and $A^T : (L^2(\Omega))^3 \to R^{3M}$, that represents the adjoint operator, is given by

$$A^T h = \left[\int_{\Omega} \Phi_1(\xi) h_1 d\xi, ..., \int_{\Omega} \Phi_M h_1 d\xi, \int_{\Omega} W_1^1(\xi) h_2 d\xi, ..., \int_{\Omega} W_M^1(\xi) h_2 d\xi, \int_{\Omega} W_1^2(\xi) h_3 d\xi, ..., \int_{\Omega} W_M^2(\xi) h_3 d\xi \right]$$

where $h = (h_1, h_2, h_3) \in (L^2(\Omega))^3$. One results:

$$A^T A = \left\| \begin{matrix} \int_{\Omega} \Phi_i \Phi_j d\xi & 0 & 0 \\ 0 & \int_{\Omega} \Phi_i \Phi_j d\xi & 0 \\ 0 & 0 & \int_{\Omega} \Phi_i \Phi_j d\xi \end{matrix} \right\|_{i,j=1}^{M} \tag{7}$$

We consider $\{\lambda_j\}_{j=1}^{3M}$ and $\{\psi_j\}_{j=1}^{3M} \subset R^{3M}$ a linear independent system of eigenvectors for $\tilde{Q}$, therefore $\tilde{Q}\psi_j = \lambda_j \psi_j$, $j = 1,...,3M$. One can see that the sequence $\{\varphi_j\}_{j=1}^{3M}$, defined by $\varphi_j = \psi_j \Phi_j$, for $1 \le j \le M$, $\varphi_j = \psi_j W_j^1$, for $M+1 \le j \le 2M$, and $\varphi_j = \psi_j W_j^2$, for $2M+1 \le j \le 3M$, represent the eigenfunctions of operator Q, i.e., $Q\varphi_j = \lambda_j \varphi_j$, $j = 1,...,3M$. The eigenfunctions of the covariance operator Q maximizes the variance of projected samples:

$$\varphi_j = arg\{max < Qh, h >_{(L^2(\Omega))^3} ; |h|_{(L^2(\Omega))^3} = 1\} \tag{8}$$

In this way the eigenfunctions $\{\varphi_j\}_{j=1}^{3M}$ capture the essential features of images from the initial training set. From $\{\varphi_j\}$ we keep a smaller number of eigenfaces $\{\varphi_j\}_{j=1}^{3M'}$, with $M' < M$ corresponding to largest eigenvalues λ_j and consider the space

$$X = lin\{\varphi_j\}_{j=1}^{3M'} \subset (L^2(\Omega))^3 \tag{9}$$

Assuming that systems $\{\varphi_j\}$ is normalized (orthonormal in $(L^2(\Omega))^3$) one can project any initial image $\{\Phi_i, W_i^1, W_i^2\} \in (L^2(\Omega))^3$ on X by formula

$$\Psi_i(x,y) = \sum_{j=1}^{3M'} \varphi_j(x,y) < \varphi_j, T_i >_{(L^2(\Omega))^3}, \; i = 1,...,3M \tag{10}$$

where $T_i = \{\Phi_i, W_i^1, W_i^2\}$, $i = 1,...,3M$ and $<\cdot,\cdot>_{(L^2(\Omega))^3}$ is the scalar product in $L^2(\Omega) \times L^2(\Omega) \times L^2(\Omega)$. We denote the weights $w_i^j = <\varphi_j, T_i >_{(L^2(\Omega))^3}$, $i = 1,...,3M$, and the resulted feature vector will be

$$V(u_i) = (w_i^1, ..., w_i^{3M}), \quad i = 1, ..., 3M \tag{11}$$

2.2 Discretization of the feature extraction approach

We discretize the continuous model described in the last section. Let us assume that $\Omega = [0, L_1] \times [0, L_2]$ and let us set $x_i = i\varepsilon, \ i = 1, ... N_2$ and $y_j = j\varepsilon, \ j = 1, ... N_1, \ \varepsilon > 0$ (Barbu, 2007).

Therefore, we obtain M matrices of size $N_1 \times N_2$, which represent the discrete images. We denote their corresponding $N_1 \cdot N_2 \times 1$ image vectors as $I_1, ..., I_M$. Now, we have $\tilde{Q} = A^T \cdot A$, where

$$A = \begin{Vmatrix} \Phi_1, ..., \Phi_M & 0 & 0 \\ 0 & W_1^1, ..., W_M^1 & 0 \\ 0 & 0 & W_1^2, ..., W_M^2 \end{Vmatrix} \tag{12}$$

and

$$\begin{cases} \Phi_k = \left\| \Phi_k(x_i, y_j) \right\|_{i,j=1}^{N_2, N_1} \\ W_k^1 = \left\| \Phi_k(x_{i+1}, y_j) - \Phi_k(x_i, y_j) \right\|_{i,j=1}^{N_2, N_1} \\ W_k^2 = \left\| \Phi_k(x_i, y_{j+1}) - \Phi_k(x_i, y_j) \right\|_{i,j=1}^{N_2, N_1} \end{cases} \tag{13}$$

The obtained matrix has a $3M \times 3M$ dimension. Thus, we determine the eigenvectors ψ_i of the matrix $\tilde{Q}$. Then, the eigenvectors of the discretized covariance operator Q are computed as following:

$$\tilde{\varphi}_i = A \cdot \psi_i, \quad i = 1, ..., M \tag{14}$$

We keep only $M' < M$ eigenimages corresponding to the largest eigenvalues and consider the space $X = linspan\{\tilde{\varphi}_i\}_{i=1}^{3M'}$. Then, the projection of $[\Phi_i, W_i^1, W_i^2]$ on X is given by the discrete version of Ψ_i, that is computed as:

$$P_X([\Phi_i, W_i^1, W_i^2]) = \sum_{j=1}^{3M'} w_i^j \cdot \varphi_j, \quad i = 1, ..., 3M \tag{15}$$

where $w_i^j = \tilde{\varphi}_j^T \cdot [\Phi_i, W_i^1, W_i^2]^T$. So, for each facial image I_i a corresponding training feature vector is extracted as the sequence of all these weights:

$$V(I_i) = [w_i^1, ..., w_i^{3M'}]^T, \quad i = 1, ..., 3M \tag{16}$$

Therefore, the feature training set of the face recognition system is obtained as $\{V(I_1),...,V(I_M)\}$, each feature vector being given by (16). The Euclidean metric could be used to measure the distance between these vectors.

2.3 Facial feature vector classification and verification

The next step of face recognition is the classification task (Duda et. al, 2000). We provide a supervised classification technique for facial authentication. Thus, we consider an unknown input image I to be recognized using the face training set $\{I_1,...,I_M\}$. The feature training set of our classifier is $\{V(I_1),...,V(I_M)\}$ and its metric is the Euclidean distance for vectors.

We normalize the input image, first. So, we get $\Phi = I - \Psi$, where $\Psi = \dfrac{1}{M}\sum_{i=1}^{M} I_i$. The vectors W^1 and W^2 are computed from Φ using formula (13). Then it is projected on the eigenspace, using the formula $P(\Phi) = \sum_{i=1}^{M} w^i \varphi_i$, where $w^i = \tilde{\varphi}_i^T \cdot [\Phi, W^1, W^2]^T$. Obviously, its feature vector is computed as $V(I) = [w^1,...,w^M]^T$ (Barbu, 2007).

A threshold-based facial test could be performed to determine if the given image represents a real face or not. Thus, if $\|P(\Phi) - \Phi\| \leq T$, where T is a properly chosen threshold value, then I represents a face, otherwise it is a non-facial image. We consider K registered (authorized) persons whose faces are represented in the training set $\{I_1,...,I_M\}$. We redenote this set as $\{I_1^1,...,I_1^{n(1)},...,I_i^1,...,I_i^{n(i)},...,I_K^1,...,I_K^{n(K)}\}$, where $K < M$ and $\{I_i^1,...,I_i^{n(i)}\}$ represents the training subset provided by the ith authorized person, $n(i)$ being the number of its registered faces.

A minimum average distance classifier, representing an extension of the classical variant of minimum distance classifier (Duda et. al, 2000), is used for feature vector classification. So, for each registered user, one calculates the average distance between its feature training subset and the feature vector of the input face. The input image is associated to the user corresponding to the minimum distance value. That user is the kth registered person, where

$$k = \underset{i}{\arg\min} \frac{\sum_{j=1}^{n(i)} d(V(I),V(I_i^j))}{n(i)} \tag{17}$$

where d is the Euclidean metric. Thus, each input face I is identified as a registered person by this formula. However, the face identification procedure has to be completed by a facial verification step, to determine if that face really represents the associated person. We propose a threshold-based verification approach.

First, we provide a novel threshold detection solution, considering the overall maximum distance between any two feature vectors belonging to the same training feature sub-set as a threshold value (Barbu, 2007). Therefore, the input face I may represent the kth registered user if the following condition is fulfilled:

$$\underset{i}{\min} \frac{\sum_{j=1}^{n(i)} d(V(I),V(I_i^j))}{n(i)} \leq T \tag{18}$$

where k is computed by (17) and the threshold is given by formula:

$$T = \max_{i} \max_{j \neq t} d(V(I_i^j), V(I_i^t))$$

(19)

If the condition (18) is not satisfied, then the input face is rejected by our recognition system and labeled as *unregistered*.

2.4 Experiments

The proposed Eigenface-based recognition system has been tested on numerous face datasets. We have performed many experiments and achieved satisfactory facial recognition results. Our technique produces a high recognition rate, of approximately 90%. We have used "Yale Face Database B", containing thousands of 192×168 face images corresponding to many persons, in our research (Georghiades et. al, 2001). In the next figures, there is represented such a face recognition example. In Fig. 1 one can see a set of 10 input faces to be recognized.

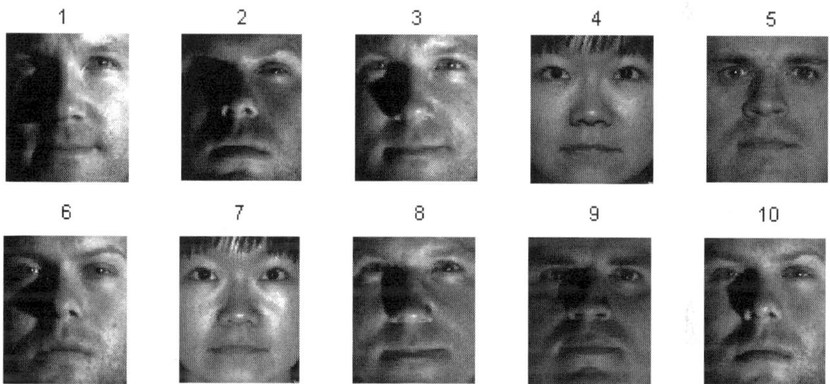

Fig. 1. Input face images

This example uses a training set containing 30 facial images belonging to 3 persons. The face set is illustrated in Fig. 2, where each registered individual has 10 photos positioned on two consecutive rows.

Therefore, one computes 90 eigenfaces for this training set but only the most important 27 ($M' = 9$) of them are necessary. The most significant eigenfaces are represented in Fig. 3. Thus, the feature training set, containing face feature vectors, is obtained on the basis of these eigenimages.

The mean distances between these feature vectors are computed and the identification process provided by (17) is applied. Faces 2, 6 and 10 are identified as belonging to the first person, faces 4 and 7 are identified to the second person. Also, the faces 5 and 9 are associated to the first registered individual but their distance values, 5.795 and 5.101, are greater than the threshold value provided by (19), computed as $T = 2.568$, so the verification procedure labels them as unregistered.

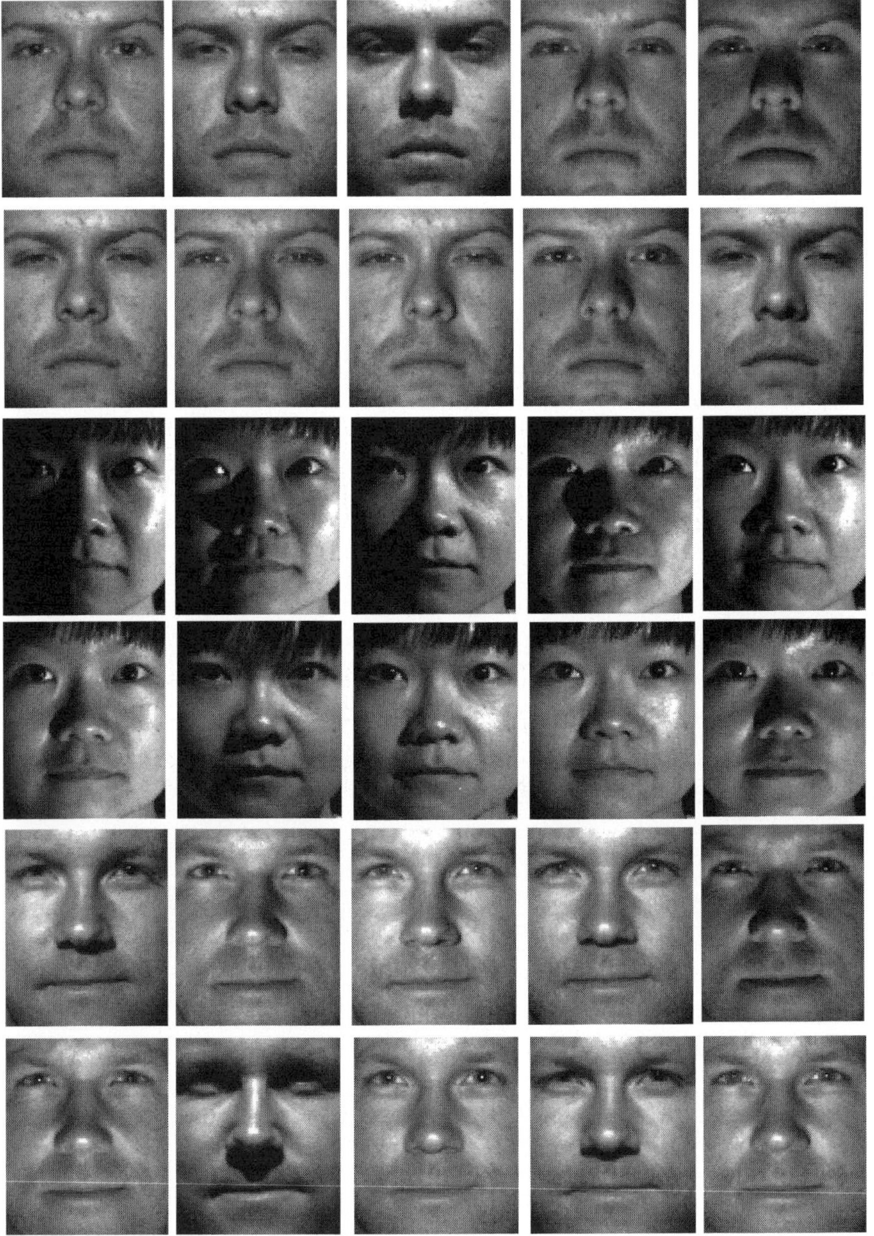

Fig. 2. Facial training set

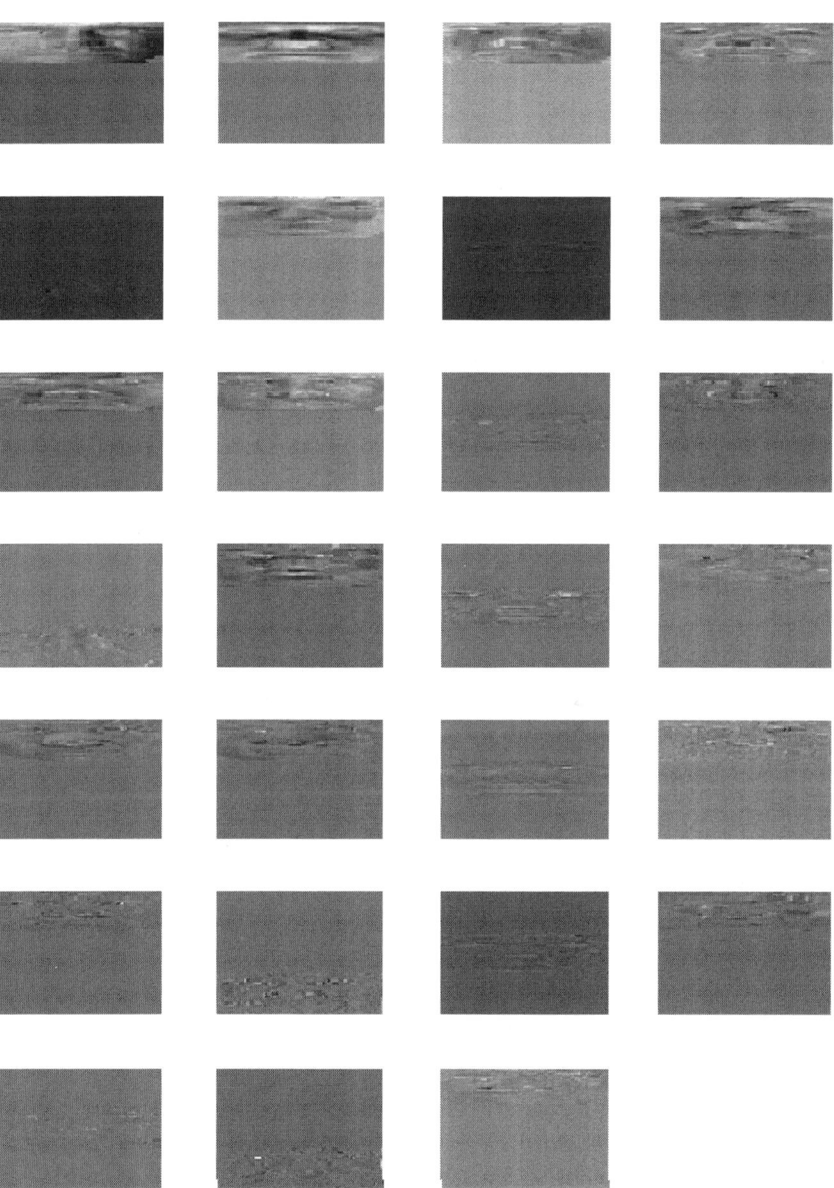

Fig. 3. The main eigenfaces

3. Face recognition technique using two-dimensional Gabor filtering

The second face authentication approach is based on two-dimensional Gabor filtering. As one knows, a great amount of research papers have been published in literature for Gabor filter-based image processing (Movellan, 2008). Besides face recognition, Gabor filters are successfully used in many other image processing and analysis domains, such as: image smoothing, image coding, texture analysis, shape analysis, edge detection, fingerprint and iris recognition.

We use the Gabor filters in the feature extraction process, that is described in the next subsection. Then, we use a feature vector classification approach that is similar to the supervised method proposed in the previous section. A threshold-based face verification is also described in the second subsection. Some facial recognition experiments are presented in the last subsection.

3.1 A Gabor filter based facial feature extraction

We intend to obtain some feature vectors which provide proper characterizations of the visual content of face images. For this reason we use the two-dimensional Gabor filtering as a feature extraction tool (Barbu, 2010).

The Gabor filter represents a band-pass linear filter whose impulse response is defined by a harmonic function multiplied by a Gaussian function. Thus, a bidimensional Gabor filter constitutes a complex sinusoidal plane of particular frequency and orientation modulated by a Gaussian envelope. It achieves optimal resolutions in both spatial and frequency domains (Movellan, 2008, Barbu, 2010). Our approach designs 2D odd-symmetric Gabor filters for face image recognition, having the following form:

$$G_{\theta_k,f_i,\sigma_x,\sigma_y}(x,y) = exp\left(-\left[\frac{x_{\theta_k}^2}{\sigma_x^2} + \frac{y_{\theta_k}^2}{\sigma_y^2}\right]\right) \cdot cos\left(2\pi f_i x_{\theta_k} + \varphi\right) \tag{20}$$

where $x_{\theta_k} = x \cos \theta_k + y \sin \theta_k$, $y_{\theta_k} = y \cos \theta_k - x \sin \theta_k$, f_i provides the central frequency of the sinusoidal plane wave at an angle θ_k with the x – axis, σ_x and σ_y represent the standard deviations of the Gaussian envelope along the axes x and y.

Then, we set the phase $\varphi = \pi / 2$ and compute each orientation as $\theta_k = \frac{k\pi}{n}$, where $k = \{1,...,n\}$. The 2D filters $G_{\theta_k,f,\sigma_x,\sigma_y}$ computed by (20) represent a group of wavelets which optimally captures both local orientation and frequency information from a digital image (Barbu, 2010).

Each facial image has to be filtered by applying $G_{\theta_k,f,\sigma_x,\sigma_y}$ at various orientations, frequencies and standard deviations. A proper design of Gabor filters for face authentication requires an appropriated selection of those parameters. Therefore, we consider some proper variance values, a set of radial frequencies and a sequence of orientations, respectively.

The settings for the filter parameters are: $\sigma_x = 2$, $\sigma_y = 1$, $f_i \in \{0.75, 1.5\}$ and $n = 5$, which means $\theta_k \in \left\{\frac{\pi}{5}, \frac{2\pi}{5}, \frac{3\pi}{5}, \frac{4\pi}{5}, \pi\right\}$. One results the filter bank $\left\{G_{\theta_k,f_i,2,1}\right\}_{f_i \in \{0.75,1.5\}, k \in [1,5]}$, that is composed of 10 channels. The current face image is convolved with each 2D Gabor filter from this set. The resulted Gabor responses are then concatenated into a three-dimensional feature vector. So, if I represents a $[X \times Y]$ face image, then the feature extraction is modeled as:

$$V(I)[x,y,z] = V_{\theta(z),f(z),\sigma_x,\sigma_y}(I)[x,y] \tag{21}$$

where $x \in [1,X]$, $y \in [1,Y]$ and

$$\theta(z) = \begin{cases} \theta_z, & z \in [1,n] \\ \theta_{z-n}, & z \in [n+1,2n] \end{cases}, \quad f(z) = \begin{cases} f_1, & z \in [1,n] \\ f_2, & z \in [n+1,2n] \end{cases} \tag{22}$$

and

$$V_{\theta(z),f(z),\sigma_x,\sigma_y}(I)[x,y] = I(x,y) \otimes G_{\theta(z),f(z),\sigma_x,\sigma_y}(x,y) \tag{23}$$

A fast 2D convolution is performed using Fast Fourier Transform, so, the face feature vector is computed as $V_{\theta(z),f(z),\sigma_x,\sigma_y}(I) = FFT^{-1}[FFT(I) \cdot FFT(G_{\theta(z),f(z),\sigma_x,\sigma_y})]$. For each face I one obtains a 3D face feature vector $V(I)$, that has a $[X \times Y \times 2n]$ dimension.

This feature vector proves to be a satisfactory content descriptor of the input face. In Fig. 4 one depicts a facial image and its 10 Gabor representations, representing the components of its feature vector.

Fig. 4. Feature vector components of a face image

The distance between these feature vectors must be computed using a proper metric. Since the size of each vector depends on the dimension of the featured image, a resizing procedure has to be performed on the face images, first. Then, we compute the distance between these 3D feature vectors using a *squared Euclidean metric*, which is characterized by formula:

$$d(V(I),V(J)) = \sum_{x=1}^{X}\sum_{y=1}^{Y}\sum_{z=1}^{2n} \left| V(I)[x,y,z] - V(J)[x,y,z] \right|^2 \tag{24}$$

where I and J are two face images, resized to the same $[X \times Y]$ dimension.

3.2 Face feature vector classification and verification

Feature vector classification represents the second step of the face identification process. We provide a similar supervised classification approach for these Gabor filter-based 3D feature vectors. Some well-known supervised classifiers (Duda et. al, 2000), such as minimum distance classifier or the *K-Nearest Neighbour (K-NN)* classifier, could be also used in this case.

The training set of this classifier is created first. Therefore, one considers N authorized system users. Each of them provides a set of faces of its own, named templates, which are included in the training set. Thus, the training face set can be modeled as $\left\{\left\{F_j^i\right\}_{j=1,...,n(i)}\right\}_{i=1,...,N}$, where F_j^i represents the jth template face of the ith user and $n(i)$ is the number of training faces of the ith user. The classification algorithm produces N face classes, each one corresponding to a registered person. Next, one computes the training vector set as $\left\{\left\{V(F_j^i)\right\}_{j=1,...,n(i)}\right\}_{i=1,...,N}$.

If the input faces to be recognized are $\{I_1,...,I_K\}$, the classification procedure inserts each of them in the class of the *closest* registered person, representing the user corresponding to the minimum *average distance*. The minimum average distance classification process is described by a formula that is similarly to (17):

$$Class(j) = arg \min_{i\in[1,N]} \frac{\sum_{t=1}^{n(i)} d(V(I_j),V(F_t^i))}{n(i)}, \forall j \in [1,K] \tag{25}$$

where the obtained $Class(j) \in [1,N]$ represents the index of the face class where I_j is introduced. Let $C_1,...,C_N$ be the resulted classes, representing the facial identification result. Next, a verification procedure is performed, to complete the face recognition task. We use a similar automatic threshold-based verification approach (Barbu, 2010). Therefore, one computes a proper threshold value as the overall maximum distance between any two training face feature vectors corresponding to the same registered user, that is:

$$T = \max_{i\leq N}\left(\max_{j\neq k\in[1,n(i)]} d\left(V(F_j^i),V(F_k^i)\right)\right) \tag{26}$$

If the average distance corresponding to an image from a class is greater than threshold T, then that image has to be rejected from the face class. The verification process is represented formally as follows:

$$\forall i \in [1,N], \forall I \in C_i : \frac{\sum_{j=1}^{n(i)} d(V(I),V(F_j^i))}{n(i)} > T \Rightarrow C_i = C_i - \{I\} \tag{27}$$

The rejected images, that could represent non-facial images or faces of unregistered users, are included in a new class C_{N+1} , labeled as *Unauthorized*.

3.3 Experiments and method comparisons

We have performed many facial recognition experiments, using the proposed Gabor filter based approach. Our recognition system has been tested on various large face image datasets and good results have been obtained.

A high face recognition rate, of approximately 90%, has been reached by our recognition system in the experiments involving hundreds frontal images. We have obtained high values (almost 1) for the performance parameters, *Precision* and *Recall*, and for the combined measure F_1 . That means our approach produce a small number of false positives and false negatives (missed hits).

We have used the same database as in the previous case, *Yale Face Database B*, containing thousands of 192×168 faces at different illumination conditions, representing various persons, for our authentication tests (Georghiades et. al, 2001). The obtained results prove the effectiveness of the proposed human face authentication approach. We have obtained lower recognition rates for images representing rotated or non-frontal faces, and higher authentication rates for frontal images.

We have performed some comparisons between the two proposed facial recognition techniques. Also, we have compared them with other face authentication methods. Thus, we have compared the performance of our approaches with the performances of Eigenface-based systems, which are the most popular in the facial recognition area.

Therefore, we have tested the Eigenface algorithm of Turk & Pentland, our Eigenface technique and the Gabor filter based method on the same facial dataset. One have computed the statistical parameters *Precision* and *Recall*, using the number of correctly recognized faces and the number of correctly rejected faces, for these approaches, the values registered in Table 1 being obtained.

	Eigenface (T&P)	Eigenface (TB)	Gabor filter based
Precision	0.95	0.85	0.88
Recall	0.94	0.85	0.90

Table 1. Performance parameter comparison

As one can see in this table, the three face recognition techniques produce comparable performance results. The original Eigenface technique performs slightly better than our two methods.

4. Conclusions

We have proposed two automatic supervised facial recognition approaches in this chapter. As one can observe, the two face authentication techniques performs the same sequence of recognition related processes: feature extraction, feature vector classification and verification of the face identity.

While the two recognition methods differ substantially in the feature extraction stage, they use quite similar classification and verification techniques. In both cases, the feature vector classification process is supervised and based on a facial training set. We propose a minimum average distance classifier that produces proper face identification. Also, both methods use a threshold-based verification technique. We have provided a threshold value detection approach for face verification.

The main contributions of this work are brought in the feature extraction stages of the proposed recognition techniques. The most important contribution is the continuous model for the Eigenface-based feature extraction. Then, the discretized version of this model represents another important originality element of this chapter.

The proposed Gabor filtering based feature extraction procedure represents another contribution to face recognition domain. We have performed a proper selection of the Gabor 2D filter parameters and obtained a powerful Gabor filter set which is successfully applied to facial images.

We have compared the two recognition methods, based on the results of our experiments, and found they have quite similar performances. Also, both of them are characterized by high face recognition rates. The facial authentication techniques described here work for cooperative human subjects only. Our future research in the face recognition domain will focus on developing some recognition approaches for non-cooperative individuals.

The recognition techniques of this type can be applied successfully in surveillance systems and law enforcement domains. A facial authentication approach that works for non-cooperative persons could be obtained by combining one of the recognition techniques proposed in this chapter with a face detection method (Barbu, 2011).

5. References

Zhao, W., Chellappa, R., Phillips, P. J. (2003). Face Recognition: A Literature Survey, *ACM Computing Surveys*, Volume 35, Number 4, pp. 399-458.

Turk, M. A. & Pentland, P. A. (1991). Face recognition using eigenfaces, *Proc. Of Computer Vision and Pattern Recognition*, pp. 586-591, IEEE.

Barbu, T. (2007). Eigenimage-based face recognition approach using gradient covariance, *Numerical Functional Analysis and Optimization*, Volume 28, Issue 5 & 6, pp. 591 – 601.

Yin, B., Bai, X., Shi, Q., Sun, Y. (2005). Enhanced Fisherface for Face Recognition, *Journal of Information and Computational Science*, No. 3, pp. 591-595.

Samaria, F., Young S. (1994). *HMM based architecture for face identification*, Image and Computer Vision, volume 12, pp. 537-583.

Wiskott, L., Malsburg, C. (1996). Face Recognition by Dynamic Link Matching, In J. Sirosh, R. Miikkulainen and Y. Choe editors, *Lateral Interactions in the Cortex: Structure and Function*. UTCS Neural Networks Research Group, Austin, TX, ISBN 0-9647060-0-8.

Barbu, T. (2010). Gabor filter-based face recognition technique, *Proceedings of the Romanian Academy*, Series A: Mathematics, Physics, Technical Sciences, Information Science, Volume 11, Number 3, pp. 277 – 283.

Barbu, V. (1998). *Partial Differential Equations and Boundary Value Problems*, Kluwer Academic Publishers, Dordrecht, Boston, London.

Duda, R. O., Hart, R. P., Stork, D. G. (2000), *Pattern Classification*. John Wiley & Sons.

Georghiades, A. S., Belhumeur, P. N., Kriegman, D. J. (2001). From Few to Many: Illumination Cone Models for Face Recognition under Variable Lighting and Pose. *IEEE Trans. Pattern Anal. Mach. Intelligence*, Vol. 23, No. 6, pp. 643-660.

Movellan, J.R. (2008). *Tutorial on Gabor filters*, http://mplab.ucsd.edu/tutorials/gabor.pdf.

Barbu, T. (2011). An Automatic Face Detection System for RGB Images, *International Journal of Computers, Communications & Control*, Vol. 6, No.1, pp. 21-32

Part 2

Feature-Based Face Detection, Analysis and Recognition Algorithms

3

Face Recognition Using Frequency Domain Feature Extraction Methods

Gualberto Aguilar, Jesús Olivares,
Gabriel Sánchez, Héctor Pérez and Enrique Escamilla
Instituto Politécnico Nacional, SEPI Culhuacan
México, D.F.

1. Introduction

The development of security systems based on biometric features has been a topic of active research during the last years, because the recognition of the people identity to access control is a fundamental issue in this day. Terrorist attacks happened during the last decade have demonstrated that it is indispensable to have reliable security systems in offices, banks, airports, etc.; increasing in such way the necessity to develop more reliable methods for people recognition. The biometrics systems consist of a group of automated methods for recognition or verification of people identity using the physical characteristics or personal behavior of the person under analysis.

In particular, face recognition is a task that humans perform carry out routinely in their daily lives. Face recognition is the most common form human beings have of telling one another apart. Faces are universal, and they provide a means to differentiate individuals. An advantage of biometric face recognition compared to other biometric is the ability to capture a facial image with a camera from a distance and without the subject's knowledge. The face recognition has been a topic of active research because the face is the most direct way to recognize the people. In addition, the data acquisition of this method consists, simply, of taking a picture with or without collaboration of the person under analysis, doing it one of the biometric methods with larger acceptance among the users. The face recognition is a very complex activity of the human brain. For example, we can recognize hundred of faces learned throughout our life and to identify familiar faces at the first sight, even after several years of separation, with relative easy. However it is not a simple task for a computer. Thus to develop high performance face recognition systems, we must to develop accurate feature extraction and classification methods, because, as happens with any pattern recognition algorithm, the performance of a face recognition algorithm strongly depends on the feature extraction method and the classification systems used to carry out the face recognition task. Thus several feature extraction methods for using in face recognition systems have been proposed during the last decades, which achieve high accurate recognition. Among the situations that drastically decrease the accuracy and that must be considered to develop high performance face recognition method we have: partial occlusion, illumination variations, size change, rotation and translation of the capture image, etc. To solve these problems several efficient feature extraction methods have been proposed, several of them using frequency domain transforms such as Discrete Gabor Transform, Discrete Cosine Transform, Discrete Wavelet Transform, etc.

The face image as biometric feature has very high intra-person variations comparing with other features, such as iris pattern and fingerprints (Reid, 2004). These variations make the face recognition a very difficult task (Chellappa, Wilson and Sirohey, 1995). However because its advantages are overcome the potential disadvantages, several face recognition algorithms have been proposed to solve the still remaining problems. Thus during the last years have been proposed template-based face recognition methods (Brunelli, Poggio, 1993), face recognition using eigenfaces methods (Turk and Pentland, 1991; Moghaddam, Wahid and Pentland, 1998), Bayesian algorithms (Chellappa, Wilson and Sirohey, 1995), geometric feature based methods (Smith, 2002; Tanaka, Ikeda and Chiaki, 1998) and Walsh transform based algorithms (Yoshida, Kamio and Asai, 2003; Shanks, 1969), etc. Other related systems that also have been applied are face region locating method proposed in (Baron, 1981), the deformable model proposed in (Lanitis, Taylor and Cootes, 1995) and face recognition methods using the Karhunen-Loeve transform (Kirby and Sirovich, 1990), etc. Recently several authors have proposed the combination of different features to improve the face recognition rate (Hallinan, Gordon, Yullie, Gablin and Mumford, 1999). On the other hand, the discrete Gabor Transform, that presents some relation with the human visual system, has been successfully used in several applications such as fingerprint enhancement (Hong, Wan and Jain, 1998), signature recognition (Cruz, Reyes, Nakano and Perez, 2004), image compression (Daugman, 1988), etc.

In this chapter, several frequency domain feature extraction methods based on the Discrete Gabor Transform, Discrete Wavelet Transform, Discrete Cosine Transform, Discrete Walsh-Hadamard Transform, Eigenfaces, and Eigenphases are analyzed. These feature extraction methods are used with different classifiers such as artificial neural networks (ANN), Gaussian Mixture Models (GMM) and Support vector machines (SVM) to evaluate each method.

2. Face recognition algorithms

The face recognition systems can perform either, face identification and identity verification tasks. In the first case the system output provides the identity of the person with highest probability, while in the second case the system determines is the person is whom he/she claims to be. In general, in both cases consists of three modules: face detection, feature extraction, and matching. Face detection separates the face area from background. Feature extraction is performed to provide effective information that is useful for distinguishing between faces of different persons. In the identification process, for face matching, the extracted feature vector of the input face is matched against those of enrolled face in the database. In the verification process, the extracted feature vector of the input face is matched against versus one feature vector. Face recognition percentages depend too much on features that are extracted to represent the input face.

2.1 Discrete Gabor transform

To estimate the features vector, firstly the NM captured image is divided in MxMy receptive fields each one of size (2Nx+1)(2Ny+1), where Nx=(N-Mx)/2Mx, Ny=(M- My)/2My. This fact allows that the features vector size be independent of the captured image size.

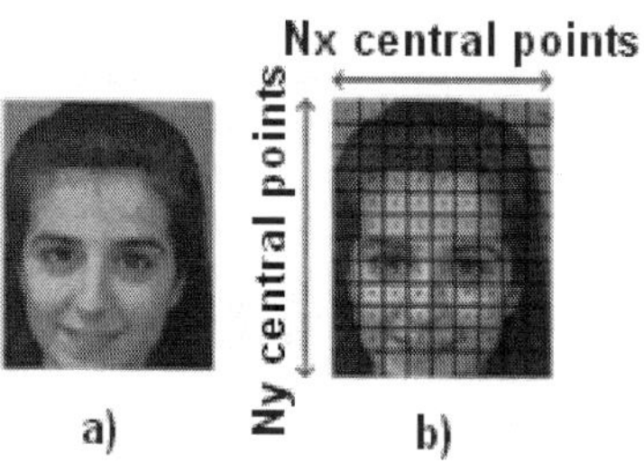

Fig. 1. a) Original image b) Nx*Ny receptive fields and central points estimation (x,y)

Next, the central point of each receptive field whose coordinates are given by (c_i, d_k), where $i=1,2,..,N_x$ y $k=1,2,3,...,N_y$, are estimated. Subsequently the first point of the cross-correlation between each receptive field and the $N\omega N\phi$ Gabor functions are estimated using eqs. (1)-(4), where $N\omega$ denotes the number of normalized radial frequencies and $N\phi$ the number of angle phases as follows:

$$w(x, y, w_m \phi_n) = g(x_n', y_n')(\cos w_m (x_n' + y_n') + j \sin w_m (x_n' + y_n'))$$ (1)

where $m=1,2,...,N\omega$ and $n=1,2,3,.., N\phi$, w_m is the m-th normalized radial frequency,

$$g(x_n', y_n') = \left(\frac{1}{2\pi\lambda\sigma^2}\right)\exp\left(-\frac{(x_n'/\lambda)^2 + y_n'^2}{2\sigma^2}\right)$$ (2)

is the Gaussian function, σ^2 is the radial bandwidth, λ is Gaussian shape factor and (x_n', y_n') is the position of the pixel (x,y) rotated by an angle ϕ_n as follows

$$(x_n', y_n') = \left((x\cos\phi_n + y\sin\phi_n), (-x\sin\phi_n + y\cos\phi_n)\right)$$ (3)

Thus the cross-correlation between the Gabor functions, given by eqs. (1)-(3), with each receptive field can be estimated as

$$h(u,v) = \sum_{x=-Nx}^{Nx} \sum_{y=-Ny}^{Ny} I(x - c_i, y - d_k)w(x, y, \omega_m, \phi_n)$$ (4)

where $u=My*(i-1)+k$ and $v=N\omega*(m-1)+n$. Next, to avoid complex valued data in the features vector we can use the fact that the magnitude of h(u,v) presents a great similarity with the behavior of the complex cells of the human visual system. Thus the magnitude of h(u,v) could be used instead of its complex value. However, as shown in eq.(4) the number of elements in the features vector is still so large even for small values of Mx, My, $N\phi$ y $N\omega$. Thus to reduce the number of elements in the features vector, we can average h(u,v) to obtain the proposed features vector M(u) which is given by

$$M(u) = \frac{1}{N} \sum_{v=1}^{Nv} |h(u,v)|$$ (5)

where Nv=NφNω. Figure 2 illustrates the results of this method. One can see that for the same person with different rotations the feature vector has a similarity, but with another person is very different.

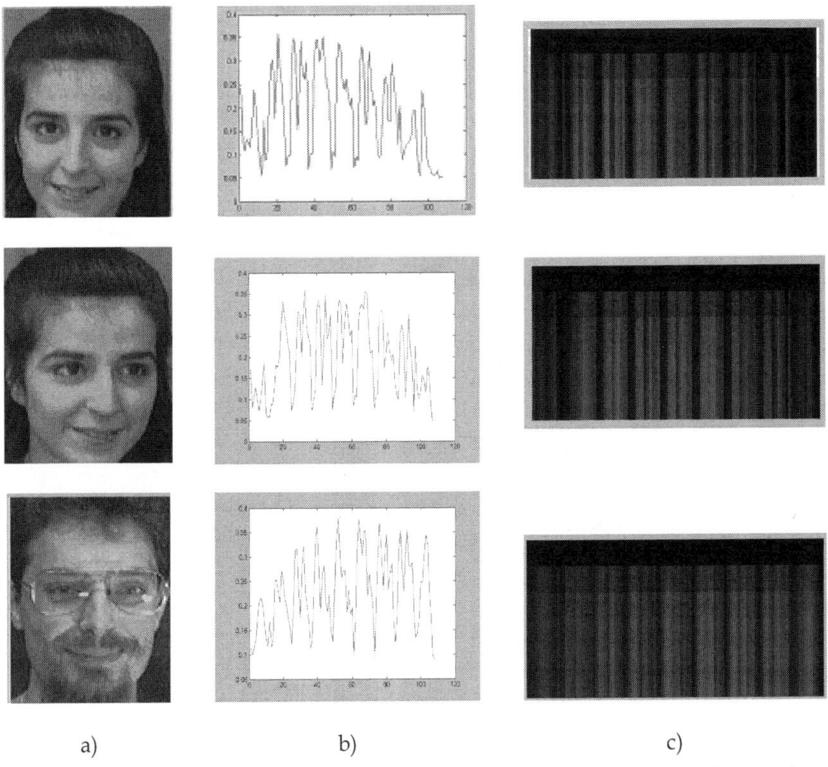

a)   b)   c)

Fig. 2. a) Original images, b) Estimated features vectors, c) Features extracted from each receptive field h(u,v).

2.1.1 Results

To evaluate this method two different databases were used. "The AR Face Database", which includes face images with several different illuminations, facial expression and partial occluded face images with transparent eyeglasses, dark eyeglasses and scarf, etc. and the "ORL database", created by Olivetti Research Laboratories in Cambridge UK. A Backpropagation neuronal network was trained with feature vectors of 50 face images and tested with feature vectors of 72 face images that were not used in the training process. To carry out the personal verification using face images with different ages, the neural network was trained with feature vectors extracted from 10 different images and evaluated using feature vectors extracted from 24 images do not used in training process. The evaluation results, under the above mentioned conditions are shown in Table 1.

Identification Percentage	Verification Percentage
85.6%	99.3%

Table 1. Results using Discrete Gabor Transform

2.2 Discrete Cosine Transform

The DCT is used in many standard image compression and stationary video as the JPEG and MPEG, because it presents excellent properties in codifying the outlines of the images that, in fact, has been one of the main reasons to be selected into almost all the coding standards. The cosine transform, like the Fourier transform, uses sinusoidal basis functions. The difference is that the cosine transform basis functions are not complex; they use only cosine functions and not sine functions (Scott, 1999). 2D DCT based features are sensitive to changes in the illumination direction (Conrad, Kuldip, 2003). The idea of using the transform for facial features extraction is summarized as follows: the given face image is analyzed on block by block basis given an image block I(x, y), where x,y = 0,1,...., Np−1, and result is an Np x Np matrix C(u,v) containing 2D DCT coefficients. The DCT equations are given by formulas (6-9) below:

$$C(u,v) = \alpha(u) \bullet \alpha(v) \bullet \sum_{x=0}^{N_p-1} \sum_{y=0}^{N_p-1} I(x,y) \bullet B(x,y,u,v) \tag{6}$$

for u,v = 0,1,2,..,Np−1 where

$$\alpha(u) = \begin{cases} \sqrt{\dfrac{1}{N}} \, for & u = 0 \\ \sqrt{\dfrac{2}{N}} \, for & u = 1,2,N-1 \end{cases}$$

$$\alpha(v) = \begin{cases} \sqrt{\dfrac{1}{N}} \, for & v = 0 \\ \sqrt{\dfrac{2}{N}} \, for & v = 1,2,N-1 \end{cases} \tag{7}$$

$$B(x,y,u,v) = \cos\left[\frac{(2x+1)u\pi}{2N}\right]\cos\left[\frac{(2y+1)v\pi}{2N}\right] \tag{8}$$

To ensure adequate representation of the image, each block overlaps its horizontally and vertically neighboring blocks by 50%, thus for an image which has Ny rows and Nx columns, there are N_D blocks found by following formula:

$$N_D = (2(Ny / Np) - 1) * (2(Nx / Np) - 1) \tag{9}$$

Compared to other transforms, DCT has the advantages of having been implemented in a single integrated circuit because of input independency, packing the most information into the fewest coefficients for most natural images, and minimizing block like appearance (Feichtinger and Strohmer, 1998; Kamio, Ninomiya, and Asai, 1994). An additional advantage of DCT is that most DCT coefficients on real world images turn out to be very small in magnitude (Feichtinger and Strohmer, 1998).

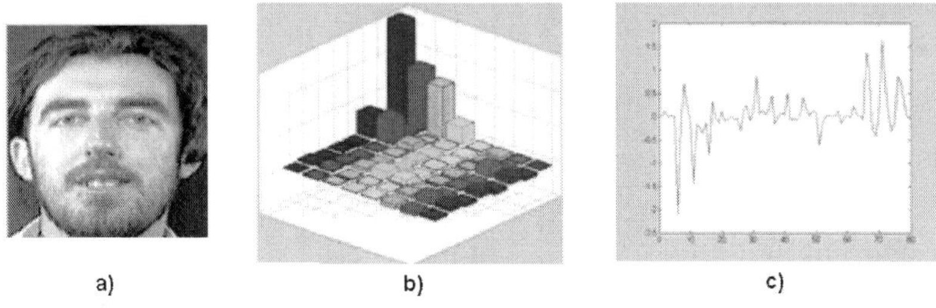

Fig. 3. a) Original image, b) Reducing image, c) Spectrum of a block, d) Feature vector

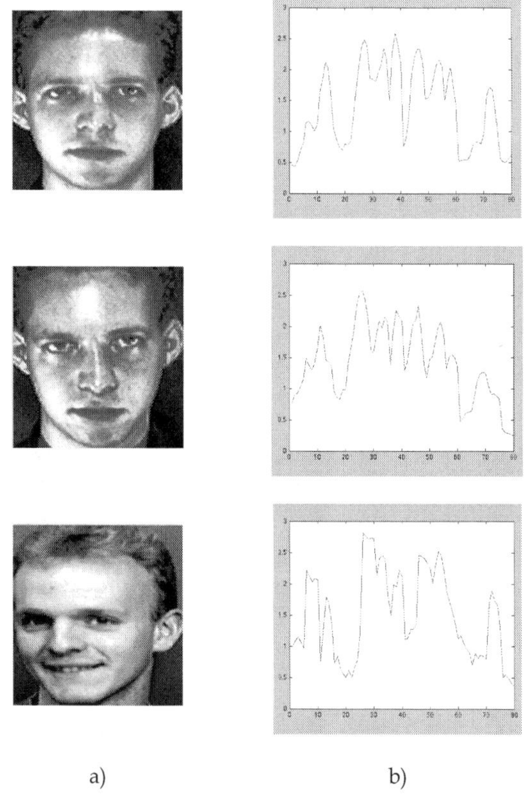

a)   b)

Fig. 4. a) Original images, b) Feature vectors.

Figure 3 shows an example. Figure 3a shows the input image. Figure 3b shows the frequency coefficients in a block of 8 x 8 and finally Figure 3c shows the characteristic vector of the face. To form the feature vector, in each block were selected the first 10 coefficients in zig-zag to be later concatenated. Figure 4 shows the feature vectors using DCT. One can see that for the same person with different distance the feature vector has a similarity, but with another person is very different.

2.2.1 Results
To evaluate this method were used the same conditions mentioned for Gabor's method. The results are shown in table 2.

Identification Percentage	Verification Percentage
79.7 %	95.1%

Table 2. Results using Discrete Cosine Transform

2.3 Discrete Walsh Transform
The discrete Walsh transform (DWT) is one of the most important techniques as well as the discrete Fourier transform in the field of signal processing (Kamio, Ninomiya and Asai, 1994; Mar and Sheng, 1973). The DWT works well for digital signals due to the fundamental function called the Walsh function. The Walsh function has only +/- 1, and is the system of orthogonal functions. In general, the Walsh function can be generated by the Kronecker's product of the Hadamard matrix H's. First, the 2-by-2 Hadamard matrix H2 is defined by

$$H_2 = \begin{bmatrix} + & + \\ + & - \end{bmatrix} \tag{10}$$

where the symbols + and – mean +1 and -1, respectively. Furthermore, calculating the Kronecker's product between two H2's, the 4-by-4 Hadamard matrix H4 is easily given as follow:

$$H_4 = H_2 \otimes H_2 = \begin{bmatrix} +H_2 & +H_2 \\ +H_2 & -H_2 \end{bmatrix} = \begin{bmatrix} + & + & + & + \\ + & - & + & - \\ + & + & - & - \\ + & - & - & + \end{bmatrix} \tag{11}$$

where the symbol $\otimes$ indicates the Kronecker's product. The Hadamard matrix can give the frequency characteristics. Along each row of the Hadamard matrix, the number of changes in sign expresses the frequency. The number of changes is called "sequence". The sequence has the characteristics similar to the frequency. The Walsh function can be expressed as each row of HN, where N is order on Hadamard matrix. Therefore, DWT is known as a kind of the Hadamard transform, where HN has some useful following characteristics. Thus, the DWT and the inverse DWT are defined as follows:

$$V = \frac{1}{N} H_N B \tag{12}$$

$$B = H_N V \tag{13}$$

where B is the sampled data vector, HN is the Hadamard matrix, i.e. Hadamard-ordered Walsh functions. V is the DWT of B. V is called Walsh spectrum. The 2D-DWT does the DWT toward the images of m-by-n pixels. The 2D-DWT and the 2D-IDWT are defined as follows:

$$F = \frac{1}{MN} H_M f H_N \tag{14}$$

$$f = H_M F H_N \tag{15}$$

where f is the sample data matrix and F is the 2D-DWT of f. F is called 2-dimensional Walsh spectrum. In case of orthogonal transform of the image, the 2D-DWT is more efficient than the DWT. However, to use 2D-DWT, the row and column numbers of sample data, matrix must be 2n (n is a natural number) respectively, because Hadamard matrix can be generated by the Kronecker's product of Hadamard matrix H2.

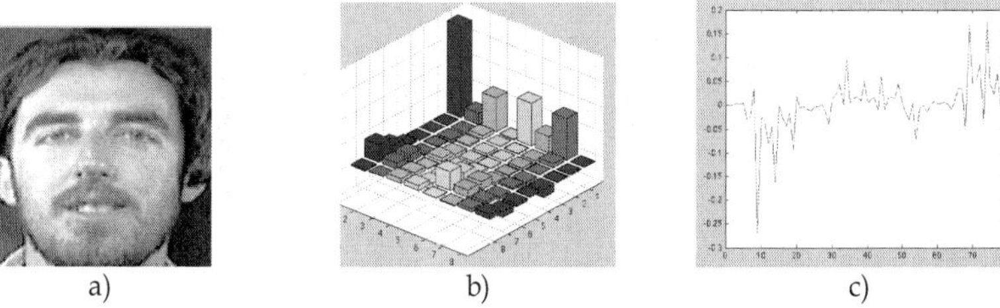

a)   b)   c)

Fig. 5. a) Original image, b) Spectrum of a block, c) Feature vector

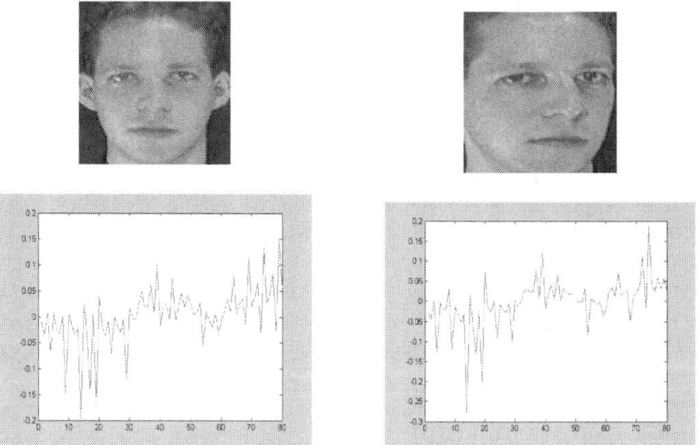

Fig. 6. Input images and features vectors of the same person.

Figure 5 shows the input image, the frequency coefficients in a block of 8 x 8 and the feature vector respectively. Figure 6 shows two images of one same person but with different rotation. The feature vectors have a very similar despite the change and the figure 7 shows that the feature vectors change significantly when the input faces are different people.

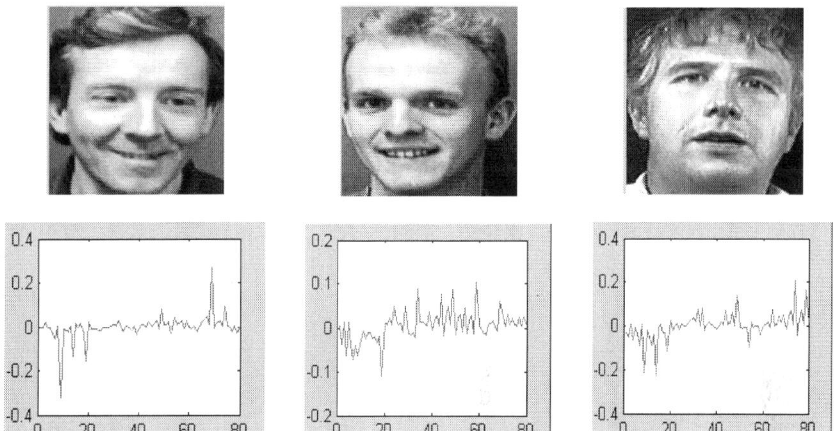

Fig. 7. Input images and features vectors of the same person.

2.3.1 Results

To evaluate this method were used the same conditions mentioned for Gabor's method. The results are shown in table 3.

Identification Percentage	Verification Percentage
76.2 %	90.3%

Table 3. Results using Discrete Walsh Transform

2.4 Eigenfaces

The objective of the recognition by the Eigenfaces method is to extract relevant information from face image, encode this information as efficiently as possible and compare them with each model stored in a database. In mathematical terms, we wish to find the principal components of the distribution of faces, or the eigenvectors of the covariance matrix of the set of face images (Smith, 2002).

The idea of using eigenfaces was motivated by a technique developed by Sirovich and Kirby (Sirovich and Kirby, 1987) for efficiently representing pictures of faces using principal component analysis. They argued that a collection of face images can be approximately reconstructed by storing a small collection of weights for each face and a small set of standard pictures.

The Eigenfaces computation is as follows: Let the training set of face images be $\Gamma_1, \Gamma_2, \Gamma_3, ..., \Gamma_M$. The average face of the set is defined by

$$\Psi = \frac{1}{M}\sum_{n=1}^{M}\Gamma_n \qquad (16)$$

Each face differs from the average by the vector

$$\phi_n = \Gamma_n - \psi \tag{17}$$

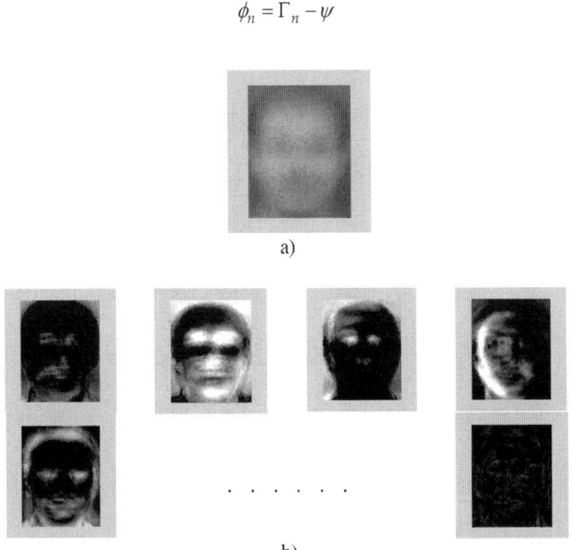

a)

b)

Fig. 8. a) Average face. b) Eigenfaces

The set of very large vectors is then subject to principal component analysis, which seeks a set of M orthonormal vectors μ_n and their associated eigenvalues λ_k which best describes the distribution of the data. The vectors μ_k and scalars λ_k are the eigenvectors and eigenvalues, respectively, of the covariance matrix

$$C = \frac{1}{M}\sum_{n=1}^{M}\phi_n\phi_n^T = AA^T \tag{18}$$

where the matrix $A = [\phi_1\phi_2...\phi_M]$, A^T is a transposed matrix. The matrix C, however, is N^2 by N^2, and determining the N^2 eigenvectors and eigenvalues is an intractable task for typical image sizes. We need a computationally feasible method to find these eigenvectors. Fortunately we can determine the eigenvectors by first solving a much smaller M by M matrix problem, and taking linear combinations of the resulting vectors.

Consider the eigenvectors v_n of A^TA such that

$$A^T A v_n = \lambda_n v_n \tag{19}$$

Premultiplying both sides by A, we have

$$AA^T A v_n = \lambda_n A v_n \tag{20}$$

from which we see that Avn are the eigenvectors of $C = AA^T$ Following this analysis, we construct the M by M matrix $L = A^TA$, where $L_{m,n} = \phi_m^T\phi_n$, and find the M eigenvectors v_n

of L. These vectors determine linear combinations of the M training set face images to form the eigenfaces u_n

$$u_n = \sum_{k=1}^{M} v_{nk}\phi_k = An_n, \quad n = 1,...,M \tag{21}$$

With this analysis the calculations are greatly reduced, from the order of the number of pixels in the images (N^2) to the order of the number of images in the training set (M). In practice, the training set of face images will be relatively small ($M<<N^2$), and the calculations become quite manageable. The associated eigenvalues allow us to rank the eigenvectors according to their usefulness in characterizing the variation among the images.

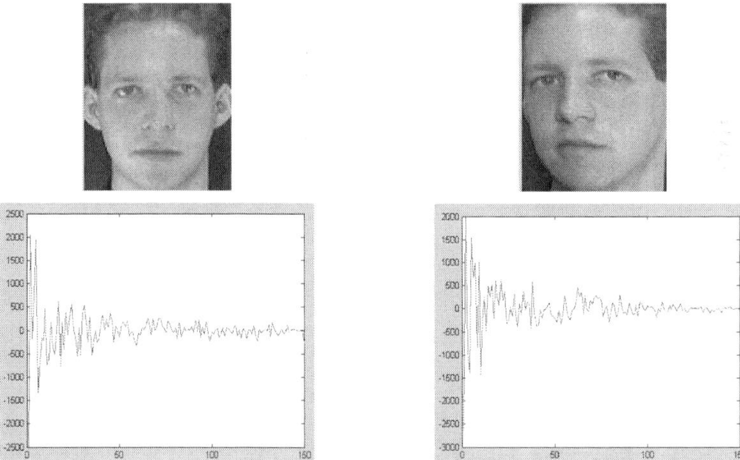

Fig. 9. Face and feature vectors of the same person.

Once the Eigenfaces have been calculated, the image is projected onto "face space" by a simple operation,

$$\omega_n = u_n(\Gamma - \Psi) \tag{22}$$

for n=1,....,M. This describes a set of point-by-point image multiplications and summations. Some Eigenfaces are shown in figure 8b.

The weights form a vector $\Omega^T = [\omega_1, \omega_2,...,\omega_M]$ that describes the contribution of each eigenface in representing the input face image, treating the eigenfaces as a basis set for face images. Finally, the simplest method for determining which face class provides the best description of an input face image is to find the face class k that minimizes the Euclidian distance

$$\varepsilon_k^2 = \left\| \Omega - \Omega_k \right\|^2 \tag{23}$$

where Ω_k is a vector describing the kth face class. Figure 9 shows the feature vectors of the same person with different rotation using the Eigenfaces method.

Figure 10 shows the feature vectors of different people using the Eigenfaces method.

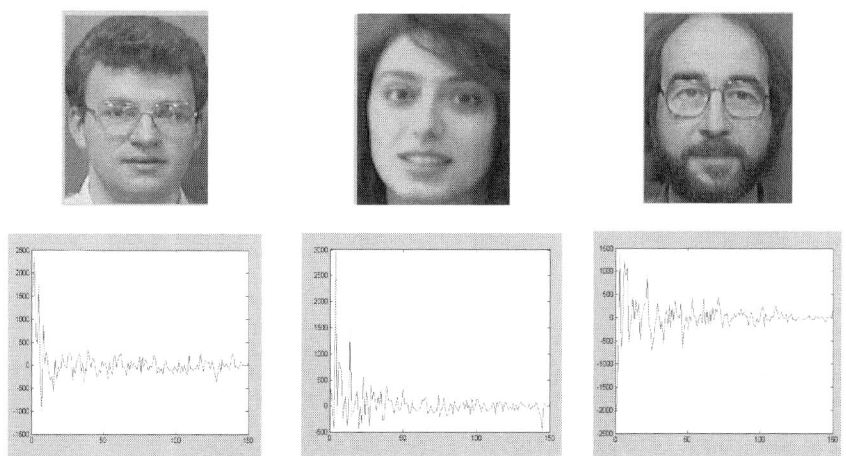

Fig. 10. Images of different people and their feature vectors.

2.4.1 Results

To evaluate this method were used the same conditions mentioned for Gabor's method. The results are shown in table 4.

Identification Percentage	Verification Percentage
83 %	99.6%

Table 4. Results using Eigenfaces

2.5 Discrete Wavelet Transform

The Discrete Wavelet Transform (DWT) is a special case of the WT that provides a compact representation of a signal in time and frequency that can be computed efficiently it is easy to implement and reduces the computation time and resources required. Wavelet transform (WT) has been widely applied to engineering fields, including signal and image processing, geophysical signal processing, computer vision and encoding, speech synthesis and analysis, signal singularity detection and spectrum estimation, pattern recognition quantum physics, hydrodynamics, fractal and chaos theory, etc. The wavelet theory adopts gradually precise step sizes of time domain or space domain for high frequency, and thus can focus on any details of an analyzed target.

The DWT of a given signal x is estimated by passing it through a series of low pass and high pass filters (Fig. 11). First the samples are passed through a low pass filter with impulse response $g(n,m)$ resulting in a convolution of the two. The signal is also decomposed simultaneously using a high-pass filter $h(n,m)$. The detail coefficients are the high-pass filter outputs and the approximation coefficients are the low-pass ones. It is important that the two filters, related to each other, are known as a quadrature mirror filter. However, since half the frequencies of the signal have now been removed, half the samples can be discarded according to Nyquist's rule. The filter outputs are:

$$Y_{LOW}(n,m) = \sum_{j=-\infty}^{\infty} \sum_{k=-\infty}^{\infty} x(n.m)g(2n-k,2m-j) \tag{24}$$

$$Y_{HIGH}(n,m) = \sum_{j=-\infty}^{\infty} \sum_{k=-\infty}^{\infty} x(n,m)h(2n-k,2m-j) \tag{25}$$

This decomposition reduces the spatial resolution since only a quarter of each filter output allows characterizing the face image. However, because each output has bandwidth equal to a quarter of the original one, the output image can be decimated to reduce the image size.

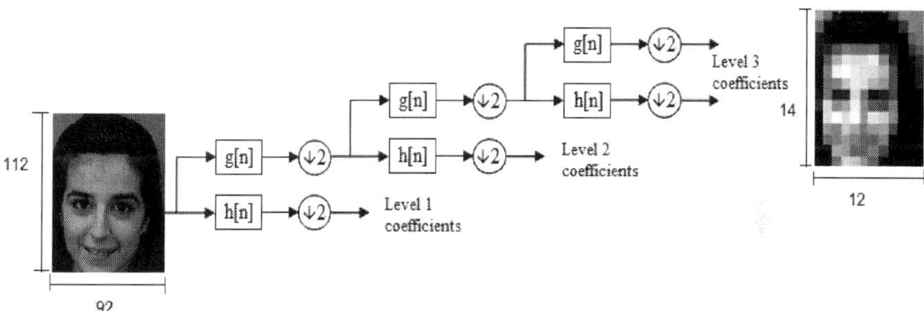

Fig. 11. 3 level wavelet decomposition

Here only the approximation coefficients are used to characterize the face image. This decomposition is repeated to further increase the frequency resolution and the approximation coefficients decomposed with high and low pass filters and then down-sampled. This is represented as a binary tree with nodes representing a sub-space with different time-frequency localization. The tree is known as a filter bank. At each level in the above diagram the signal is decomposed into low and high frequencies. Due to the decomposition process the input signal must be a multiple of 2n where n is the number of levels.

2.5.1 Results

To evaluate this method was used a SVM classifier. The feature vectors of training images obtained as mentioned above are applied to a SVM to obtain the optimal model of each class; these models are used in the classification stage. Where the input of each one is the feature vector of the face to classify and the output is an approximation of each model.

Since the support vector machine is a supervised system, it needs a smaller amount of information in the training stage to obtain a model capable of separating the classes successfully.

To evaluate this methods "The AR Face Database" was used, which has a total of 5,670 face images of 120 people (65 men and 55 women) that includes face images with several different illuminations, facial expression and partial occluded face images with sunglasses and scarf. The training set consists of images with and without occlusions, as well as illumination and expressions variations. Here the occlusions are a result of using sunglasses and scarf. These images sets and the remaining images of the AR face database are used for testing. The results are shown in table 5.

Identification Percentage	Verification Percentage
92.5 %	99.2%

Table 5. Results using Discrete Wavelet Transform

2.6 Eigenphases

Oppenheim et al (Oppenheim, 1981) have shown that phase information of an image retains the most of the intelligibility of an image. This is also demonstrated by Oppenheim's experiment shown in Figure 12.

Their research also shows that given just the phase spectrum of an image, one can reconstruct the original image up to a scale factor, thus phase information is the most important in representing a 2D signal in the Fourier domain. We have taken two face images; one from person 1 and one from person 2 as shown. The Fourier transform of both images were computed, and the respective phase spectrum and magnitude spectrum were extracted. We then synthesized new frequency array using the phase spectrum of person 1 combined with the magnitude spectrum from person 2. Similarly we took the phase spectrum from person 1 and combined it with the magnitude spectrum of person 2. We observe, that the synthesized face images closely resemble the face image from which the corresponding phase spectrum was extracted from, thus supporting the proposition that phase spectrum contains most of the intelligibility of images.

Since we have established that the complex phase spectrum contains most of the image information, it seems logical to seek to model the image variation by modeling the variation in the phase spectrum of a given sequence of training images.

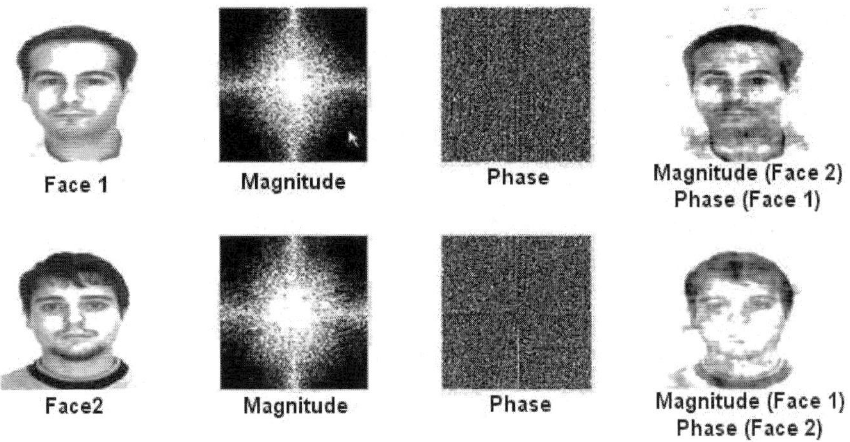

Fig. 12. Oppenheim's experiment.

To perform the face classification task, a PCA (Smith, 2002) is used to obtain the main characteristics of the faces training. Figure 13 shows the process:

Image 1, Image 2...Image N in Figure 13 are the phase spectrum of the training faces. In training phase, basis vectors are obtained by PCA. In the testing phase, the basis vectors obtained in training phase are used to extract the features for a classifier.

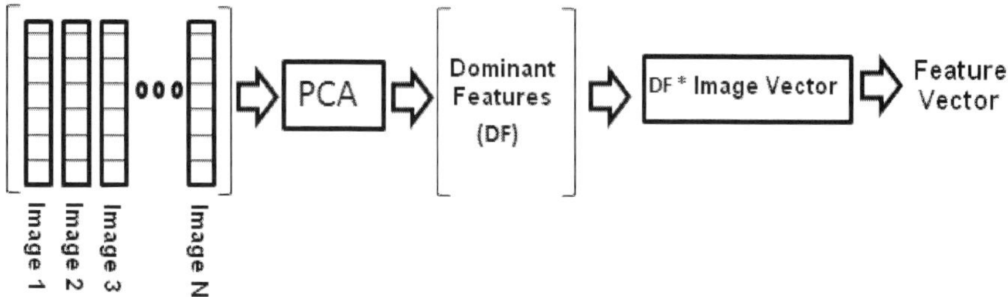

Fig. 13. Feature extraction by PCA

This method per- forms well although the recognition performance can be de- graded in the presence of illumination variations and partial face occlusions.

Figure 14 shows the features vector obtained using Eigenphases. The vectors of the same person with different illumination show similitude.

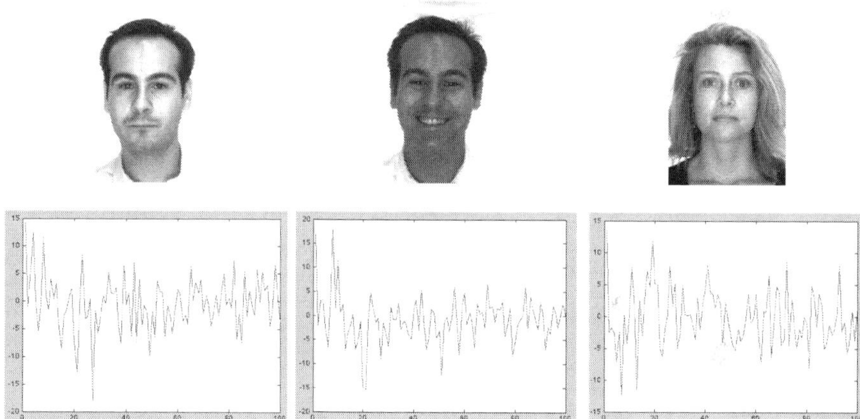

Fig. 14. Features vectors.

In this method a histogram equalization stage was proposed. Histogram equalization is a method in image processing for contrast adjustment. This method usually increases the global contrast of many images, especially when the usable data of the image is represented by close contrast values. Through this adjustment, the intensities can be better distributed on the histogram. The method is useful in images with backgrounds and foregrounds that are both bright and dark.

Histogram equalization was performed in 5 different ways:

Global equalization of the image and obtain the phase spectrum of the complete image (Global EQ)

Perform a local equalization of the image using windows of size 3 × 3 and obtain the phase spectrum of the complete image (Local 3)

Perform a local equalization of the image using windows of size 6 × 6 and obtain the phase spectrum of the complete image (Local 6)

Equalization of the image and estimate the phase spectrum locally using windows of size 3 × 3 (Local Fourier 3)
Equalization of the image and estimate the phase spectrum locally using windows of size 6 × 6 (Local Fourier 6)
The histogram equalization is obtained by:

$$p_r = (r_k) = \frac{n_k}{MN} \quad k = 0,1,2,...,L-1 \tag{26}$$

where p_r is the probability that an intensity occurs rk, n_k is the number of times the pixel with intensity k appearing in the picture and M and N is the number of rows and columns in the original image. To compute the output of the histogram equalization, the following equation is used:

$$s_k = (L-1)\sum_{j=0}^{k} p_r(r_j) \quad k = 0,1,2,...,L-1 \tag{27}$$

where L is the gray scale.

2.6.1 Results
To evaluate this method were used the same conditions mentioned for Wavelet's method. The results are shown in table 6.

Identification Percentage	Verification Percentage
87.5 %	99%

Table 6. Results using Eigenphases

Method	Identification Percentage	False acceptance	False reject
E.G	87.24 %	0.07%	4.66%
Local 3	87.58 %	0.03%	7.65%
Local 6	86.95 %	0.01%	8.93%
Local Fourier 3	89.57%	0.29%	0.8%
Local Fourier 6	89.37%	0.68%	0.52%

Table 7. Results using Histogram equalization

3. Conclusion

In this chapter several frequency domain feature extraction methods were analyzed. The feature vectors are then fed into a classifier, for example a multilayer neural network (ANN), Gaussian Mixture Models (GMM) or Support vector machines (SVM) to recognize the face image.
A modification to the Eigenphases algorithm was proposed based on the Histogram Equalization and the Phase Spectrum of an image. Also a method that allows that the features vector size can be independent of the captured image size was proposed for Gabor method.

The evaluation of some methods for feature extraction show that the some vectors are robust against changes in illumination, wardrobe, facial expressions and additive noise, blurred images (filters), resizing, shifting and even with some age changes. Therefore, the identity verification system could verify correctly the input face images with different illumination level, different facial expression, with some accessories, as well as when the face images pass through some common image processing such as filtering, contamination by noise and geometrical transformation (rotating, shifting, resizing).

The combination of methods to obtain the feature vector, such as Gabor and Eigenfaces, could deliver a higher percentage of recognition. Finally, we can emphasize some advantages of the Frequency Domain Feature Extraction Methods: Compact extraction of the face information, easy implementation, robustness against several condition changes and fast processing.

4. Acknowledgment

We thanks to the National Science and Technology Council of Mexico (CONACyT) and the IPN for financial support provided us for the realization of this research.

5. References

P. Reid. (2004). Biometrics for Networks Security. Prentice Hall, New Jersey.

R. Chellappa; C. Wilson, and S. Sirohey. (1995). Human and Machine Recognition of Faces: A Survey. Proc. IEEE, vol. 83, No. 5, pp. 705- 740.

R. J. Baron. (1981). Mechanisms of human facial recognition, International Journal of Man-Machine Studies, pp. 137-178.

L. Sirovich and M. Kirby. (March 1987). Low-dimensional procedure for the characterization of human faces," J. Opt. Soc. Am. A., Vol. 4, No. 3, pp. 519-524.

Brunelli R., Poggio T. (1993). Face recognition: Features vs. Templates. IEEE Transactions on Pattern Analysis and Machine Intelligence, Vol. 15, No. 10.

M. Turk and A. Pentland. (1991). Eigenfaces for Recognition. J. Cognitive Neuroscience, vol. 3, no.1.

M. Turk and A. Pentland. (1991). Face Recognition using Eigenfaces. Proc. IEEE Conf. on Computer Vision and Pattern Recognition, pp. 586-591.

Moghaddam B.; Wahid W. & Pentland A. (1998). Beyond eigenfaces: Probabilistic matching for face recognition. Proceedings of the Second International Conference on Automatic Face and Gesture Recognition, Nara, pp. 30-35.

I. Smith. (February 2002). A tutorial on Principal Components Analysis.

Tanaka H.T., Ikeda M and Chiaki H. (1998). Curvature-based face surface recognition using spherical correlation – Principal directions for curved object recognition. Proceedings of the Second International Conference on Automatic Face and Gesture Recognition, Nara, pp. 372-377.

M. Yoshida, T. Kamio and H. Asai. (2003). Face Image Recognition by 2- Dimensional Discrete Walsh Transform and Multi-Layer Neural Network. IEICE Trans. Fundamentals, Vol. E86-A, no.10, pp. 2623- 2627.

Shanks, J. L. (1969). Computation of the Fast Walsh-Fourier Transform," IEEE Trans. Comput., Vol. 18, No. 5, pp. 457-459.

Lanitis A., Taylor C.J. and Cootes T.F. (1995). A unified approach to coding and interpreting face images. Proceedings of the International Conference on Computer Vision ICCV'95, Cambridge.

Kirby M. and Sirovich L. (1990). Application of the Karhunen-Loeve procedure for the characterization of human faces. IEEE Transactions on Pattern Analysis and Machine Intelligence, Vol. 12, No. 1.

P. Hallinan, G. Gordon, A. Yullie, P. Gablinand and D.Mumford. (USA 1999). Two and Three Dimensional Patterns of Face.

I. Hong, Y. Wan and A. Jain. (August 1998). F°ingerprint image enhancement algorithm and performance evaluation," IEEE Trans. on Pattern Analysis and Machine Intelligence, vol. 20, No.8, pp. 777-789.

C. Cruz, R. Reyes, M. Nakano-Miyatake and H. Perez-Meana. (June 2004). Verificacion de firmas usando la transformada de Gabor," Revista Internacional Informacion Tecnologica, Vol. 15, No. 3, pp. 53-60.

J. G. Daugman. (July 1988). Complete discrete 2D Gabor transform by neural networks for image analysis and compression", IEEE Trans. on Acoustic Speech and Signal Proc., vol. 36, No. 7, pp. 1169-1179.

Scott E. (1999). Computer Vision and Image Processing. Prentice Hall PTR, Prentice Hall,Inc,Upper Saddle River,NJ 07458,ISBN :0-13-264-599-8.

Conrad S. and Kuldip K. (2003). Fast Features for Face Authentication Under Illumination Direction Changes. Pattern Recognition Letters 2, 2409-2419.

H. Feichtinger, T. Strohmer. (USA 1998). Gabor Analysis Algorithms. Ed. Birkhauser, Boston, Ma.

T. Kamio, H. Ninomiya, and H. Asai. (Nov. 1994). A neural net approach to discrete Walsh transform. IEICE Trans. Fundamentals, vol.E77-A, no.11. pp.1882-1886.

H.T.L. Mar and C.L. Sheng. (1973). Fast Hadamard transform using the H diagram. IEEE Trans. Comput., vol.C-22, No.10, pp.957-960.

A. V. Oppenheim and J. S. Lim. (May 1981). The importance of phase in signals. Proc. IEEE, vol 69, No°5, pp. 529-541.

Lindsay I Smith. (February 2002). A tutorial on Principal Components Analysis.

Local Feature Based Face Recognition

Sanjay A. Pardeshi and Sanjay N. Talbar
R.I.T., Rajaramnagar and S.G.G.S. COE &T, Nanded
India

1. Introduction

A reliable automatic face recognition (AFR) system is a need of time because in today's networked world, maintaining the security of private information or physical property is becoming increasingly important and difficult as well. Most of the time criminals have been taking the advantage of fundamental flaws in the conventional access control systems i.e. the systems operating on credit card, ATM etc. do not grant access by "who we are", but by "what we have". The biometric based access control systems have a potential to overcome most of the deficiencies of conventional access control systems and has been gaining the importance in recent years. These systems can be designed with biometric traits such as fingerprint, face, iris, signature, hand geometry etc. But comparison of different biometric traits shows that face is very attractive biometric because of its non-intrusiveness and social acceptability. It provides automated methods of verifying or recognizing the identity of a living person based on its facial characteristics.

In last decade, major advances occurred in face recognition, with many systems capable of achieving recognition rates greater than 90%. However real-world scenarios remain a challenge, because face acquisition process can undergo to a wide range of variations. Hence the AFR can be thought as a very complex object recognition problem, where the object to be recognized is the face. This problem becomes even more difficult because the search is done among objects belonging to the same class and very few images of each class are available to train the system. Moreover different problems arise when images are acquired under uncontrolled conditions such as illumination variations, pose changes, occlusion, person appearance at different ages, expression changes and face deformations. The numbers of approaches has been proposed by various researchers to deal with these problems but still reported results cannot suffice the need of the reliable AFR system in presence of all facial image variations. A recent survey paper (Abate et al., 2007) states that the sensibility of the AFR systems to illumination and pose variations are the main problems researchers have been facing up till.

2. Face recognition methods

The existing face recognition methods can be divided into two categories: holistic matching methods and local matching methods.The holistic matching methods use complete face region as a input to face recognition system and constructs a lower dimensional subspace using principal component analysis (PCA) (Turk & Pentland, 1991), linear discriminant analysis (LDA) (Belhumeur et al., 1997) , or independent component analysis (ICA) (Bartlett et al., 2002). The query face image is then projected into this subspace and matched with nearest face image on the basis of distance criterion. Recently, local matching methods are gaining more importance for face recognition application (Mandal et al., 2006; Zhang et al., 2005;, Ersi & Zelek, 2006; Kisku et al., 2007; Luo et al., 2007) because of the following reasons

1. It represents face image by a set of low dimensional local feature vectors and hence reduces computational cost and storage requirement.
2. The extracted local feature vectors are distinctive and invariant to many kinds of geometric and photometric transformations. Hence good face description can be obtained with few training samples.
3. It recognizes a face based on its parts; hence the common and class-specific features can be easily identified.
4. The use of face specific features increases classifier diversity and hence improves face recognition rate.
5. The problem of imprecise localization can be avoided by using proper feature matching algorithm such as voting based algorithm.

The general idea of local matching methods is to first locate several facial features and then classify the faces by comparing and combining the corresponding local statistics. The comparison of holistic and local matching methods given by (Heisele et al., 2003) shows that local matching methods are superior to holistic matching methods. The detection of local features can be done by local appearance based methods or local feature based methods. The local appearance based methods detects feature points by segmenting the image into sub regions. But since the performance of current image segmentation techniques are still limited, performance of recognition using local appearance based methods is limited too. However, this problem can be solved easily with local feature based methods because it forms the database of local features, each representing a unique object and during recognition, local features for an object are matched with the features stored in the database. Since images of the same object can be taken in different environmental and instrumental conditions, they are probably different but related. A difference between these images occurs due to noise level, change in illumination, scaling, rotation and change in viewing angle. In order to match such images, local features should be invariant to these differences. Thus success of local feature based methods depends largely on correct detection of local features which are highly distinctive and invariant to different imaging conditions.

The comparison of various face recognition methods, given in Table 1, confirms that local matching methods (LGBPHS and Person specific SIFT) outperform holistic matching methods. It is also evident from table that the performance of local appearance based method is better as compared to local feature based methods but the results are reported with certain restrictions and local feature based method have a potential to overcome these restrictions.

The restrictions are as follows:

1. The performance of local appearance based methods depends largely on proper image segmentation. But image segmentation is a very hard problem in itself and requires a high-level understanding of the image content. However, local feature based methods detects most discriminative feature points in the image and operates on them. Hence it does not require image segmentation.
2. The results of local appearance based methods largely depend on proper image registration which is again very difficult in presence of occlusion and geometric and photometric transformations. It is not required in local feature based methods.

3. The dimensionality of feature vector is very less in local feature based methods as compared to local appearance based method because optimum number of feature points required for image representation can be determined.

Variation / Distance metric	Expression	Illumination	Session	Time
Holistic matching method (Bartlett et al., 2002)	83.85%	64.95%	42.66%	28.21%
Local appearance based methods (Zhang et al., 2005)	94%	97%	----	68%
Local feature based Methods (Luo et al., 2007)	97%	47%	61%	53%

Table 1. Recognition rates comparison

2.1 Local feature based methods

Three important stages involved in local feature based methods are feature detection, feature description and feature matching.

2.1.1 Feature detector

The objective of this stage is to detect feature points of the image which are highly distinctive and invariant to different imaging conditions. The 2-D image windows, where there is some form of 2-D texture likes corner, are the most distinctive image patches compared with other types of image windows. The (Mikolajczyk & Schmid, 2002), presented evaluation of various feature point detectors and found that the performance of Harris detector is better for variations in scale, rotation, illumination, view point changes and image blur. However the repeatability of Harris detector degrades significantly when the images have large-scale changes. In order to cope with such changes, scale space representation of Harris detector is useful such as relative scale Harris detector or Harris-Laplace detector.

2.1.2 Feature descriptor

The objective of this stage is to describe detected feature points with the help local image statistics. A number of techniques for representing local image patch have been reported in the literatures such as differential descriptors (Mikolajczyk & Schmid, 2002), complex filters (Schaffalitzky & Zisserman, 2002), moment invariants (Van gool at el., 1996) and SIFT (Lowe,2004). The experimental evaluation of these descriptors is given by (Mikolajczyk, 2004) and it shows that SIFT descriptor provide best matching results. However, SIFT descriptor have high dimensionality and is also computationally expensive and can be replaced with Gabor filters. The (Zou at el.,2007) presented comparative study of local matching approach for face recognition and showed that good recognition rate can be obtained with Gabor features. This is possible because Gabor filter can detect changes in object location, scale, and orientation and these properties of Gabor filters make invariant detection of object possible, but in addition, Gabor filters also establish a significant degree of robustness to photometric disturbances, such as illumination change and image noise, and to natural image variations, such as backgrounds.

2.1.3 Feature descriptor matching

In most face recognition applications, there are many classes, but very few training samples are available per class and it makes difficult to estimate the parameters of sophisticated classifiers. In the view of this difficulty, the simple nearest neighbor classifier is usually adopted. The key to classification then is the similarity or distance function. Many similarity measures for both histogram and vector features have been proposed and studied in (Beveridge at el., 2004; Rubner at el., 2001). But in local matching approaches, faces are partitioned into local components and an unavoidable question is how to combine these local components to reach the final classification. Nearly all of the existing local matching methods choose to concatenate local features into single global feature before classification. An alternative approach for combining local features is to let them act as individual classifiers and then combine these classifiers for final decision. Many classifier combination methods have been studied in the literature, from static combiners, such as majority vote, sum rule, and Borda count to trainable combiners, including logistic regression and AdaBoost (Friedman at el., 2000;, Ho at el., 1994;, Kittler at el., 1998).

3. Local feature based face recognition algorithms

The three different algorithms are implemented for AFR and each of these algorithm consist of three stages i.e. feature point detector, feature point descriptor and classifier. The each algorithm is developed with different feature point detector and classifier to get reliable face recognition algorithm. The details of these algorithms and their performances in terms of recognition rate achieved for illumination, pose and expression variations as well as average recognition rate are given in sections 3.1 to 3.4.

3.1 Algorithm 1

The algorithm consist of three stages i.e. feature point detection with Harris corner detector, feature extraction with 2-D Gabor filters and feature matching with nearest neighbor classifier. The steps of the proposed algorithm given by (Pardeshi & Talbar,2006) are

1. Detect important facial feature points by application of Harris corner detector to given face image.
2. Perform segmentation of facial region from non-facial region with skin color based face segmentation algorithm. It is useful to remove the feature points detected on image background, neck, hair etc. and retain face-specific feature points.
3. Group the retained feature points into 14-clusters. The number of clusters used is 14 assuming: 2 clusters for forehead (left side and right side), 2 clusters for ears (left and right ear), 4 clusters for eyes corners (left and right corners of each eye), 2 clusters for nose corners, 2 clusters for mouth corners and 2 clusters for chin corners. After clustering, each cluster center is used as feature point.
4. Extract image local information from these feature points with 2-D Gabor filters. The Gabor filters are designed for 4-scales and 4-orientations and it results in total 16 masks. Each Gabor mask is centered at feature point and convolved with local image patch of size 25 × 25. The magnitude value of each convolution is used to construct a feature

vector. Since each feature point is convolved with 16 Gabor masks, the resulting feature vector has a size of 1 × 16.

5. Concatenate the feature vectors extracted from 14 feature points to form single global feature vector of size 1 × 224.

6. In training phase, apply PCA to global feature vectors extracted from all training images and build an eigenspace.

7. During recognition phase, project the global feature vector extracted from test image, by application of all steps mentioned in 1 to 5, into eigenspace.

8. Check image similarity in eigenspace with six different distance metrics i.e. city-block distance (L1 norm), Euclidian distance (L2 norm), Cosine distance (COS), Mahalanobis distance (MAH), sum of L1 and MAH distance (L1 + MAH) and sum of L2 and MAH distance (L2 + MAH). The image with shortest distance to test image will be considered as a best match.

3.1.1 Feature point detector

The Harris corner detector analyzes the auto-correlation matrix M of every location in an image that is computed from image derivatives as given in equation (1):

$$M = g(\sigma_I) * \begin{bmatrix} I_x^2(X) & I_x I_y(X) \\ I_x I_y(X) & I_y^2(X) \end{bmatrix} \tag{1}$$

here X is pixel location vector, $I_x(X)$ is x-gradient at location X, $I_y(X))$ is y-gradient at location X and $g(\sigma_I)$ is Gaussian kernel of scale σ_I. A point is located as a corner if

$$R = \text{Det}(M) - K \times Trace(M)^2 = I_x^2 I_y^2 - (I_x I_y)^2 - K \times (I_x + I_y)^2 \tag{2}$$

here K is an empirical constant ranged from 0.04 to 0.06. The repeated detection of same corner point in local neighborhood of feature point is avoided by setting threshold and ensuring that feature point has maximum value of R in its local neighborhood as

$$R(X) > R(X_w) \forall X_w \in W \wedge R(X) > thershold \tag{3}$$

here W denotes the 8-neighbors of the point X. The result of application of Harris corner detector to one of the subject of Asian Face database is shown in image displayed as Fig.1.

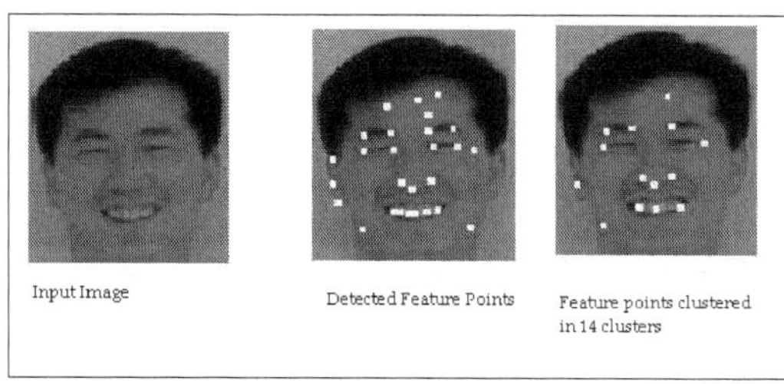

Fig. 1. Feature Point Detector Stage

It shows input image, detected feature points and result of clustering. The all feature points are shown by highlighting its 3 × 3 neighborhood for the purpose of visibility. It is evident from figure that feature points are detected at eyebrow corners, eye corners, nose corners, mouth corners and chin i.e. at locations where signal changes in both directions simultaneously. These points carry highly discriminative information and used as feature points.

3.1.2 Feature extraction

The 2-D Gabor filters are used for feature point description. The Gabor filters enhances low level image features such as the peaks, valleys and ridges so that the eyes, the nose and the mouth, as well as the other salient local features like dimples are get enhanced. These key features are important for discrimination of different faces. A family of complex Gabor filters is defined as

$$W(x,y) = \ell^{-\frac{x'^2+\gamma^2 y'^2}{2\sigma^2}} \cos\left(2\Pi\frac{x'}{\lambda}+\varphi\right) \tag{4}$$

$$\text{where } x' = x\cos\theta + y\sin\theta \text{ and } y' = -x\sin\theta + y\cos\theta$$

here θ: Orientation, λ: wavelength of cosine wave, φ: phase of sinusoid, σ: radius of the Gaussian and γ: aspect ratio of the Gaussian. The Gabor filter bank is designed for 4-scales (λ) and 4-orientations (θ) and it results in total 16 Gabor filters. The values of λ and θ used are

$$\lambda\epsilon\left(4,4\sqrt{2},8,8\sqrt{2}\right) \text{ and } \theta\epsilon\left(0,\frac{\pi}{4},\frac{\pi}{2},\frac{3\pi}{4}\right) \tag{5}$$

To extract a feature vector, each Gabor filter mask of size 25×25 is placed at selected feature point and convolved with local image patch centered at feature point. The magnitude values of these convolutions are used to get feature vector of size 16×1 for each feature point. All these feature vectors extracted from feature points are concatenated to get final global feature vector. Since each image is represented by 14 feature points and each feature point is represented by feature vector of size 16×1, global feature vector has size of 224×1 as

$$x^i = \left[x_1^i \ldots\ldots\ldots\ldots\ldots x_N^i\right]^T where\ N = 224, i = subject \tag{6}$$

The Asian face database is used to carry out various experiments. This database consists of true-color face images of 103 people, out of that 53 are men and remaining 50 are women. This dataset is divided into training dataset and test dataset. The images from training dataset are used for training of algorithm while images from test dataset are used for checking the results. For each training image, single global Gabor feature vector is extracted and these vectors are placed, side-by-side, to create a data matrix X of size N × P (where N=224 × 1 is size of global feature vector and P = number of persons used for training) as

$$X = [x^1|x^2|\ldots\ldots\ldots\ldots\ldots x^P] \tag{7}$$

3.1.3 Feature vector dimensionality reduction

The dimensionality of data matrix X is very high i.e. 224 × P and is reduced further by PCA technique. The PCA is used to obtain the low dimensional representation of the data contained in data matrix while retaining as much information (energy) from the original data matrix as possible. For this mean centered feature vector $\bar{x}^i$ is obtained as

$$\bar{x}^i = x^i - m \quad where\ m = \frac{1}{p}\Sigma_{i=1}^p x^i \tag{8}$$

The mean centered data matrix $\bar{X}$ is obtained as

$$\bar{X} = \left[\overline{x^1}\,\middle|\,\overline{x^2}\,\middle|\, \ldots\ldots\ldots\ldots\ldots\ldots\,\middle|\,\overline{x^p}\right] \tag{9}$$

The $\bar{X}$ is multiplied by its transpose to get the covariance matrix as

$$\Omega = \bar{X}\bar{X}^T \tag{10}$$

The eigenvectors and eigenvalues of the covariance matrix Ω are calculated as

$$\Omega V = \Lambda\, V \tag{11}$$

here v is the set of eigenvectors associated with the eigenvalues Λ. The eigenvectors $v_i \in v$ are ordered according to their corresponding eigenvalues $\lambda_i \in \Lambda$ from high to low because eigenvector associated with largest eigenvalue represent greatest variation in features and eigenvector associated with smallest eigenvalue represent small variation in features. Finally, each mean centered feature vector is projected into eigenspace as

$$\tilde{x}^i = V^T \bar{x}^i \tag{12}$$

3.1.4 Recognition

The face recognition is done by projecting the test image, to be recognized, into eigenspace and then checking its similarity by nearest neighbor classifier. To achieve this, test image is subjected to all steps mentioned in section 3.1 to get global feature vector $\mathcal{Y}$. It is then subtracted from mean vector of data matrix (m, as calculated in equation 8), referred as $\overline{\mathcal{Y}}$, and projected into same eigenspace defined by v as

$$\tilde{y} = V^T \bar{y} \tag{13}$$

The projected test image is compared to every projected training image in eigenspace and the closest training image is selected based on minimum distance criterion

3.1.5 Distance criterion

The distance between training image and test image is calculated with six distance metrics as proposed by (Moon &Phillips, 2001) and given by equations 14 to 19.
1.   City-block distance (L1 norm):

$$d(x,y) = |x - y| = \sum_{i=1}^{k}|x_i - y_i| \tag{14}$$

2.   Squared Euclidian distance (L2 norm):

$$d(x,y)=\|x\text{-}y\|^2 = \sum_{i=1}^{K}\left(x_i - y_i\right)^2 \tag{15}$$

3.   Cosine distance (COS):

$$d(x,y) = -\frac{x.y}{\|x\|\|y\|} = -\frac{\sum_{i=1}^{k} x_i y_i}{\sqrt{\sum_{i=1}^{k} x_i^2 \sum_{i=1}^{k} y_i^2}} \tag{16}$$

4.   Mahalanobis distance (MAH):

$$d(x,y) = \sum_{i=1}^{k} x_i\, y_i\, \frac{1}{\sqrt{\lambda_i}} \quad \text{with } \lambda_i = \text{eigenvalues of i}^{\text{th}}\text{ eigenvector} \tag{17}$$

5.   Sum of L1 and Mahalanobis distance (L1+MAH):

$$d(x,y)=\sum_{i=1}^{k}|x_i y_i|\ \frac{1}{\sqrt{\lambda_i}} \tag{18}$$

6.   Sum of L2 and Mahalanobis distance (L2+MAH):

$$d(x,y)=d(x,y)=\sum_{i=1}^{k}\left(x_i - y_i\right)^2\ \frac{1}{\sqrt{\lambda_i}} \tag{19}$$

3.1.6 Test dataset

A well-designed Korean Face Database (KFDB) is used to check the algorithm performance. The database consists of images of 640 × 480 pixel resolution, 24-bit color depth and is stored in BMP and JPEG formats. It consist images of 56 male subjects and 51 female subjects with 17 variations: one frontal face image with natural expression; 4 illumination variations; 8 pose variations and 4 expression variations. The illumination variations are obtained by changing lighting directions and illumination color. The lighting direction is changed by using circular arrangement of 8-light sources separated by interval of 45^0 and illumination color variation is achieved by using fluorescent light and glow light. The pose variations are obtained by capturing the images with 7-different cameras, one camera is placed at center to capture frontal image and remaining 6-cameras are placed with 3-cameras to left side of center camera and 3-cameras to right side of center camera. The cameras on left side and right side are separated by interval of 5^0, 10^0 and 15^0 with respect to center camera to achieve total variation of 15^0 on either side of center camera. The four expression variations are also provided as Happiness, Anger, Blink and Surprise with 2-illumination colors.

The experiments are carried out to report recognition rates for three categories of test images i.e. illumination variation, pose variation and expression variation. In addition, average recognition rate is also calculated by taking average of recognition rates obtained for illumination, pose and expression variations. For each variation, one frontal face image and 50% of images of respective variation category are used for training and remaining 50% images of respective variation category are used for testing. It result in gallery and probe dataset with sizes as mentioned in Table 2.

	Probe category		
	Illumination variations	Pose variations	Expression variations
Gallery Size	168	280	168
Probe set size	112	224	112

Table 2. Sizes of gallery dataset and probe dataset for three variations

3.1.7 Experimental results and analysis

The (Moon &Phillips, 2001) carried out various experiments for design of PCA based holistic face recognition system and concluded that

- Illumination normalization as pre-processing step improves recognition rate.
- The good recognition rate can be obtained by using only first 40% eigenvectors or by removing 1st eigenvector from face representation.

- The COS is good distance metric to measure image similarity in eigenspace.

However, these results are reported for FERET database with holistic PCA based face recognition system. But, algorithm under consideration is local feature PCA based face recognition and database is also different i.e. Asian face database. Hence it is very much essential to check the applicability of these results to the algorithm under consideration. This is done by conducting similar experiments on Asian face database with proposed algorithm. Total four experiments are conducted to check recognition rates for illumination, pose and expression variations with six different distance metrics.

The first experiment is conducted as per the steps mentioned in section 3.1 and is referred as "baseline algorithm". The second experiment is performed by using illumination normalization as pre-processing step to baseline algorithm and is referred as "illumination normalization as pre-processing step". The third experiment is conducted with illumination normalization and by using only first 40% eigenvectors for face representation. It is referred as "first 40% eigenvectors". The last experiment is carried out with illumination normalization and by removing first eigenvector from face representation. It is referred as "removal of 1st eigenvector". The comparison of results obtained for illumination variation is shown graphically in Fig.2. It shows that maximum recognition accuracy of 76.25% is obtained by using illumination normalization as pre-processing step with COS distance metric. Thus illumination normalization as pre-processing step is helpful to improve the performance of proposed algorithm but use of first 40% eigenvectors for image representation or removal of 1st eigenvector from image representation actually reduces the performance.

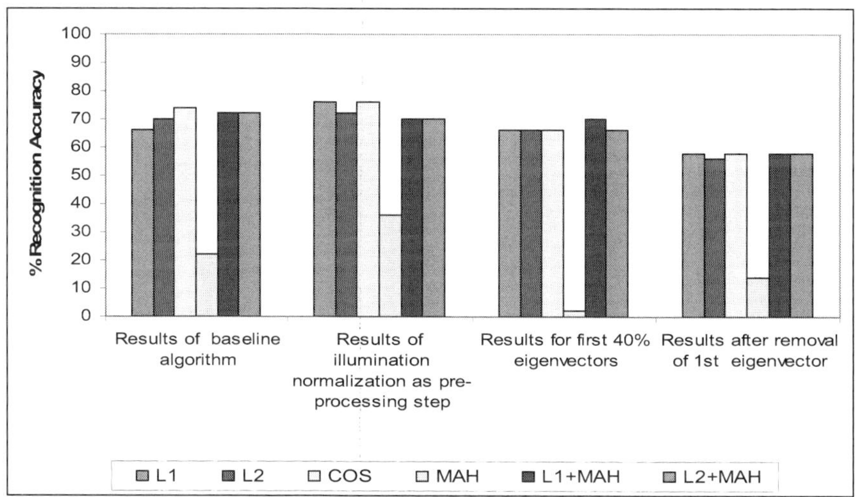

Fig. 2. Comparison of recognition rates obtained for illumination variation: Algorithm 1

The similar comparison for pose variation is shown in Fig. 3 and it shows that recognition rate of 72.5% can be obtained by using illumination normalization as pre-processing step with COS distance metric or by using 40% eigenvectors for image representation with L2 and COS distance metrics or by removing 1st eigenvector with L1 distance metric. Hence selection of proper distance metric it is very difficult.

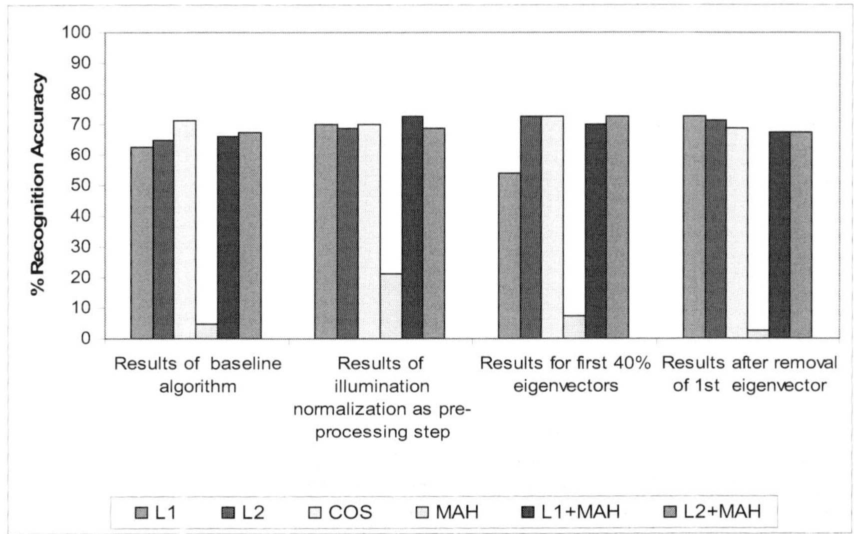

Fig. 3. Comparison of recognition rates obtained for pose variation: Algorithm 1

The graphical representation of comparison for recognition rates obtained for expression variation is shown in Fig 4. The comments of pose variation are also applicable to expression variation and maximum recognition rate achieved is 67.5%.

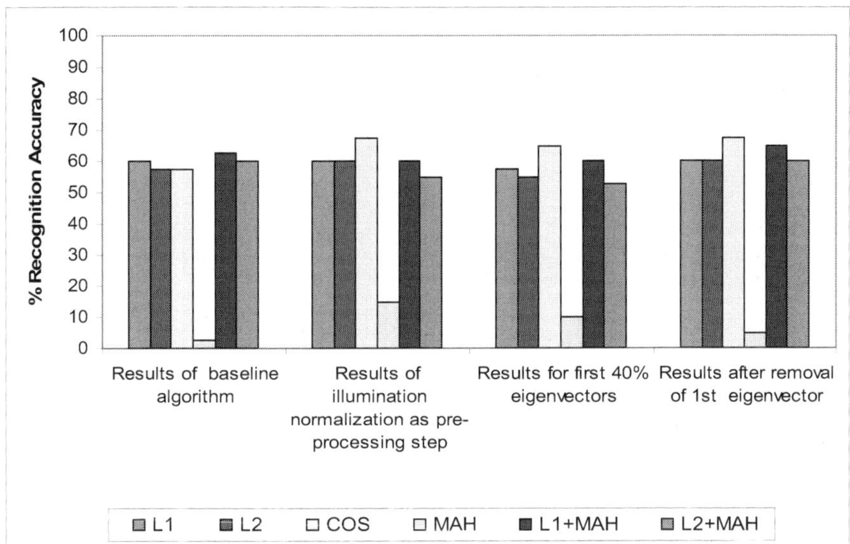

Fig. 4. Comparison of recognition rates obtained for expression variation: Algorithm 1

It is clearly evident from above comparison that it very difficult to select most suitable distance metric which works well in presence of all image variations. This problem is solved by comparing average recognition rates and its comparison is shown graphically in Fig. 5. It is evident from this comparison that maximum recognition rate of 70% can be achieved with proposed algorithm. Further it also shows that use of illumination normalization as preprocessing step is useful to improve the performance of local feature based face recognition algorithm and cosine distance metric is most suitable to measure image similarity in eigenspace.

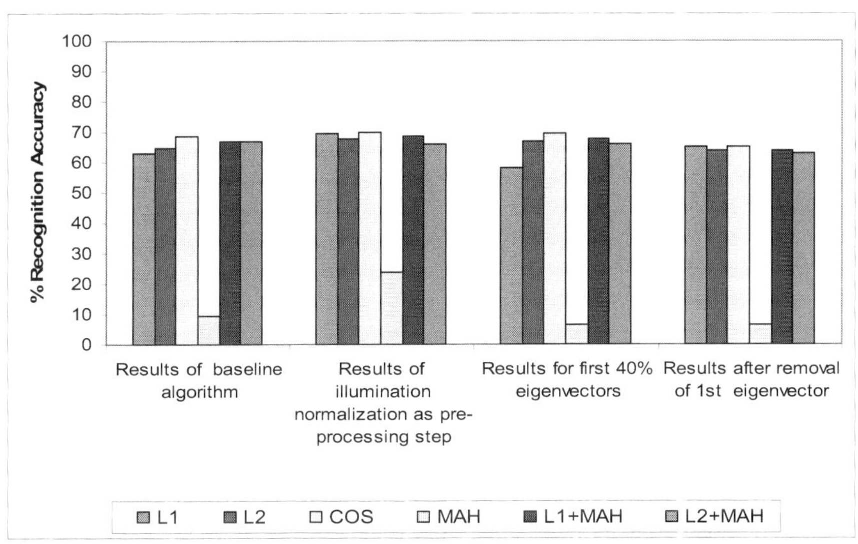

Fig. 5. Comparison of average recognition rates: Algorithm 1

3.1.8 Limitations

The recognition rates achieved with the Algorithm 1 are limited and required to be improved further. The recognition rate for expression and pose variations can be improved by making the process of feature point detection scale invariant. The reason for this is that Harris corner detector detects the feature point invariant to image rotation, scale change, illumination variation, viewpoint changes and imaging system noise but still the range is very limited. In addition, the number of feature points used to represent face image are only 14 and required to be increased further because representing the entire face image by only 14 feature points does not provide enough discrimination power to the classifier.

3.2 Algorithm 2

It is similar to Algorithm 1 except feature point detection is done with relative scale Harris detector. The steps of the proposed algorithm as given by (Pardeshi & Talbar, 2008) are
1. Illumination normalization of gray scale version of the original color face image so that normalized face image have zero mean and unity standard deviation.

2. Detect important facial feature points by application of relative scale Harris detector to given face image.
3. Perform segmentation of facial region from non-facial region with skin color based face segmentation algorithm.
4. Selection of required number of feature points based on their stability and magnitude of Harris corner response.
5. Extract image local information from these feature points with 2-D Gabor filters as mentioned in Algorithm 1.
6. Concatenate the feature vectors extracted from all feature points to form single global feature vector.
7. In training phase, apply PCA to global feature vectors extracted from all training images to build the eigenspace.
8. During recognition phase, project the global feature vector extracted from test image, by application of all steps mentioned in 1 to 6, into eigenspace.
9. Check image similarity in eigenspace with three distance metrics i.e. L1 norm, L2 norm and COS. The image with shortest distance to test image will be considered as a best match.

3.2.1 Feature point detector

The Harris corner detector, used in Algorithm 1, is not invariant to large scale changes and hence hampers correct detection of feature points in presence of pose and expression variations. To make Harris corner detector scale invariant, the scale-space representation of Harris corner detector can be explored. The idea behind this is that real-world objects are composed of different structures at different scales i.e. real-world objects may appear in different ways depending on the scale of observation. Hence to identify and select interesting image components, it is required to observe them at appropriate scale. The scale-space representation of Harris corner detector is given by (Islam at el., 2005). It allows detection of stable feature points in presence of rotation, scale change, intensity scaling, background clutter and partial occlusion. It uses relative scale σ_I as the variance of Gaussian for Harris integration while variance of Gaussian for Harris differentiation is given by $\sigma_D = K\sigma_I$, where k is a constant. The scale normalized auto-correlation matrix of Harris detector at a point $X = (x, y)$ of the image I is given as

$$N(X, \sigma_I) = \sigma_D^2 g(\sigma_I) \otimes \begin{bmatrix} I_x^2(X, \sigma_D) & I_x I_y(X, \sigma_D) \\ I_x I_y(X, \sigma_D) & I_y^2(X, \sigma_D) \end{bmatrix} \tag{20}$$

$g(\sigma_I)$ is the circular Gaussian integration window at the scale σ_I and given by

$$g(\sigma_I) = \frac{1}{2\pi\sigma_I^2} e^{-\frac{x^2+y^2}{2\sigma_I^2}} \tag{21}$$

$I_x(X, \sigma_D)$ and $I_y(X, \sigma_D)$ are given by

$$I_x(X, \sigma_D) = h(\sigma_D) \otimes I(x) \ \ and \ \ I_y(X, \sigma_D) = (h(\sigma_D))^T \otimes I(x) \tag{22}$$

here $h(\sigma_D)$ is the 1-D Gaussian first derivative kernel at the scale of σ_D defined as

$$h(\sigma_D) = -\frac{x}{\sigma_D^3 \sqrt{2\pi}} e^{-\frac{x^2}{2\sigma_D^2}} \tag{23}$$

The measure of corner response at the point X and scale σ_l is

$$R(X, \sigma_1) = \det\big((N(X, \sigma_1))\big) - \lambda tr^2(N(X, \sigma_1))$$ (24)

where λ is a constant. The point is selected as a corner point if

$$R(X, \sigma_1) > 0 \ \ and \ \ R(X, \sigma_1) > R(X_w, \sigma_1) \forall X_w \in W$$ (25)

here W is the 3×3 neighborhood of the point X. To build the scale-space representation as mentioned in (20), pre-selected scales are used with $\sigma_n = k^n \sigma_0$; σ_0 is the initial scale factor set to 1; factor k is scale factor between successive scale levels (set to 1.4 as mentioned in (Lowe, 1999), n give number of resolution levels. The matrix $N(X, \sigma_l)$ is computed with $\sigma_l = \sigma_n$ and $\sigma_D = s\sigma_n$, where S $\in$ [0.7,0.8, …1.4]. The large scale change of 1.4 is used to detect initial interest points i.e. k=1.4 and n =1 and then small scale changes, specified by s, are used to observe the detected interest points at various scales.

It detects large number of feature points, representing important image contents, at various resolution levels. But as scale changes, the spatial location of feature point changes slightly and it result in detection of same image structure at various resolution levels. To avoid this feature points are selected on the basis of its stability and strength. The feature point is said to be stable if same feature point is detected at every level of the scale while strength of the feature point is judged on the basis of magnitude of its corner response. These feature points are further sorted in descending order of their corner responses because larger corner response represents larger bidirectional signal variation at that point and hence indicate the presence of discriminant information at that point. The experiments are carried out with different number of feature points and recognition rate is checked with the objective to decide optimum number of feature points required to get good recognition rate. The detected feature points based on criterion of stability and out of these selected 30 feature points based on their corner strength are shown in Fig. 6. The feature points are superimposed on original image and 3×3 neighborhood of the feature point is highlighted for proper visibility. The remaining details of this algorithm are similar to Algorithm 1 as mentioned in 3.1.2 to 3.1.6.

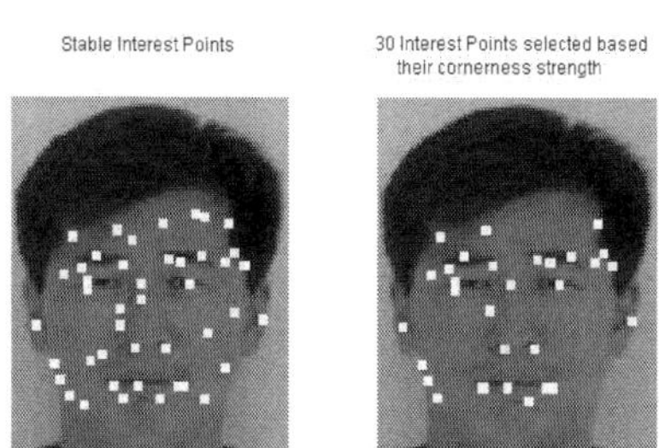

Fig. 6. Feature Point Detector Stage

3.2.2 Experimental results and analysis

The experiments are conducted to determine recognition rates obtained for illumination, pose and expression variations. These experiments are conducted by using 10, 20 and 30 feature points with the intention to determine optimum number of feature points required for face representation. The maximum number of feature points used for experimentation is only 30 because very few feature points satisfies the criterion of stability. The comparison of results obtained for illumination variation is shown graphically in Fig.7. It shows that maximum recognition accuracy of 72% is obtained by using 30 feature points with L1 and COS distance metrics. It also shows that recognition rate increases with number of feature points.

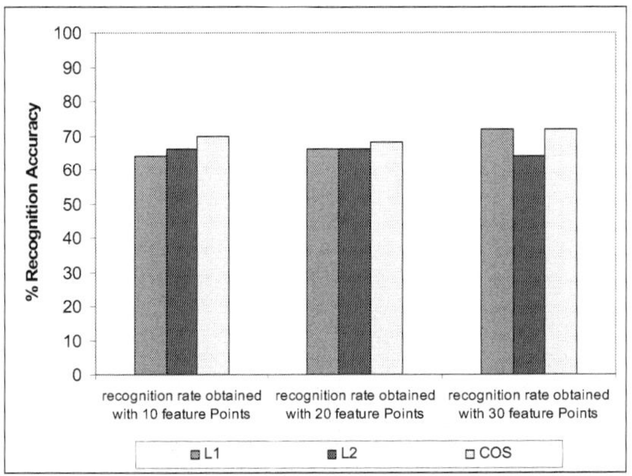

Fig. 7. Comparison of recognition rates obtained for illumination variation: Algorithm 2

The similar comparison for pose variation is shown in Fig. 8. It shows that maximum recognition rate of 72.5% is obtained by using 20 feature points with L2 and COS distance metrics and also by using 30 feature points with all distance metrics. The graphical representation of comparison for recognition rates obtained for expression variation is shown in Fig 9. It is evident that the recognition rate achieved with 30 feature points and L2 distance metric is excellent. These comparisons show that algorithm performance increases with number of feature points. But performances of distance metrics are not consistent.

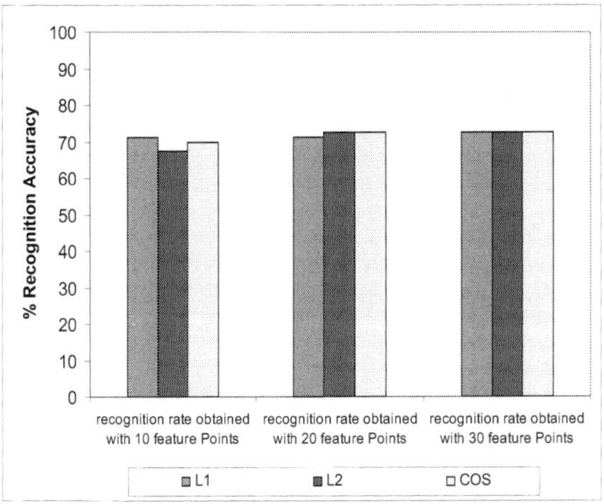

Fig. 8. Comparison of recognition rates obtained for pose variation: Algorithm 2

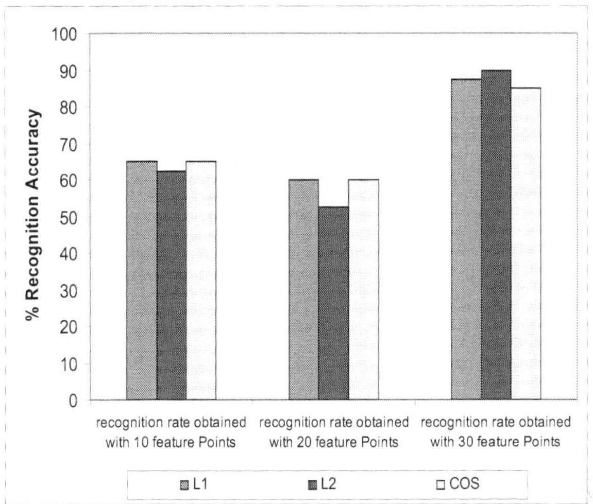

Fig. 9. Comparison of recognition rates obtained for expression variation: Algorithm 2

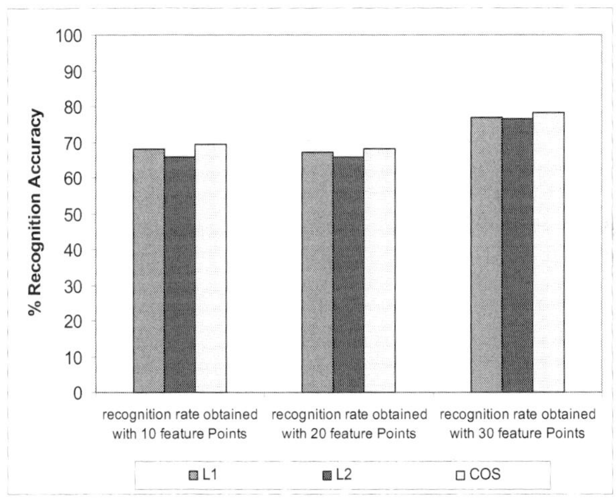

Fig. 10. Comparison of average recognition rates: Algorithm 2

To solve this problem, average recognition rates are compared and shown graphically in Figure 10. It shows that maximum recognition rate of 78.24 % can be achieved by using 30 feature points with COS distance metric.

3.2.3 Limitations
It is observed that the recognition rate increases with number of feature points used for face representation and possibility is there to increase the recognition rate further if more

After detection of feature points, feature extraction from these feature points is done as described in section 3.1.2 of Algorithm 1 while details of test dataset and gallery dataset are mentioned in section 3.1.6 of Algorithm 1. The training of the algorithm and recognition of test image is done by two classification techniques i.e. Classifier1 and Classifier2.

3.3.2 Classifier 1

The classification technique is similar to technique used in Algorithm 1 and Algorithm 2 and details of the implementation is described in sections 3.1.3 to 3.1.5 of Algorithm 1. The PCA is used for dimensionality reduction of feature vectors followed by measuring image similarity in eigenspace with three different distance metrics. The experiments are conducted with different number of feature points i.e. 50, 75,100,125 and 150 for face representation. The main intention to conduct these experiments is to determine optimum number of feature points required to achieve good recognition rate and to determine how recognition rate varies with number of feature points.

3.3.3 Classifier 1-experimental results and analysis

The experiments are conducted to determine recognition rates obtained for illumination, pose and expression variations. The comparison of results obtained for illumination variation is shown graphically in Fig.12. It shows that maximum recognition rate of 78% is obtained by using 125 feature points with L1 distance metric. The similar comparison for pose variation is shown in Fig. 13. It shows that maximum recognition rate of 82.5% is obtained by using 125 feature points with L1 and L2 distance metrics. Since performance of two distance metrics is similar, it is very difficult to select proper distance metric to measure image similarity in eigenspace. The graphical representation of comparison for recognition rates obtained for expression variation is shown in Fig 14. It shows that maximum recognition rate of 85% is obtained by using 125 feature points with COS distance metric. All these experiments confirm that optimum number of feature points required to get good recognition rate are 125. But performances of distance metrics are not consistent and it is very difficult to select one particular distance metric which works well with all types of image variations. To solve this problem, average recognition rates are compared.

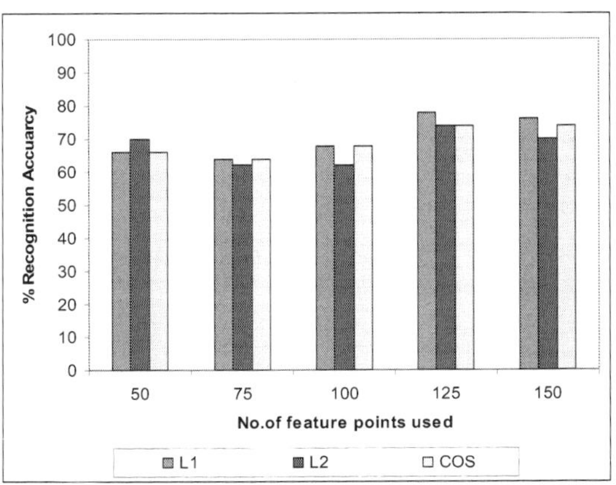

Fig. 12. Recognition rates obtained for illumination variation: Algorithm 3- Classifier1

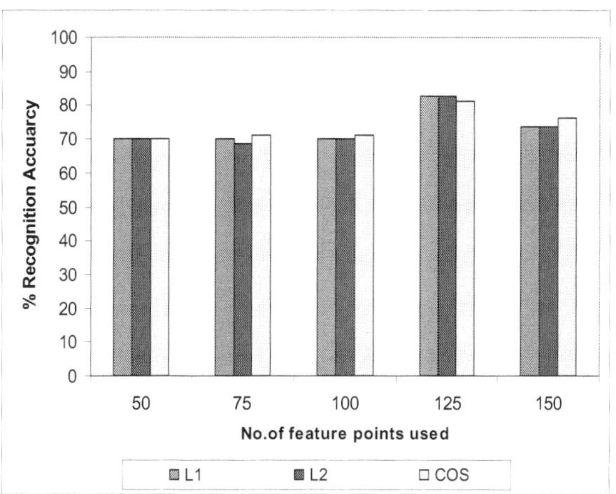

Fig. 13. Recognition rates obtained for pose variation: Algorithm 3- Classifier 1

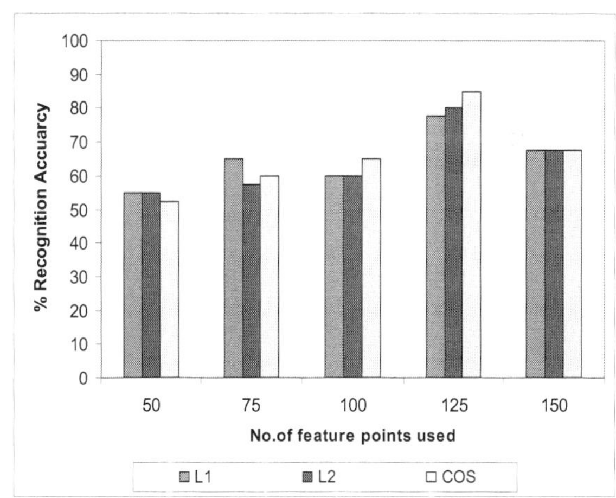

Fig. 14. Recognition rates obtained for expression variation: Algorithm 3- Classifier 1

The comparison of average recognition rates is shown graphically in Figure 15. It shows that recognition accuracy of 80% can be obtained in presence of all image variations by using 125 feature points with L1 and COS distance metric. Thus it is very difficult to select correct distance metric by comparison of average recognition rate also.

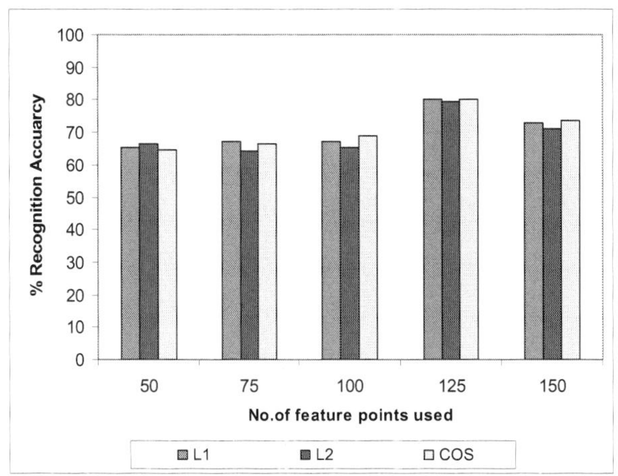

Fig. 15. Comparison of average recognition rates: Algorithm 3- Classifier 1

3.3.4 Classifier 2

The voting based classifier is used to solve the problem of inconsistent performance of various distance metrics. It classifies each feature vector individually and again combines results of individual classifiers, based on voting mechanism, to get final classification result. The reference database is generated by using images from gallery dataset (model images). The extracted feature vectors from each model image are stored in a reference database, along with a pointer to the model image from which they originate i.e. Gabor feature vector extracted from K^{th} feature point of ith reference face is stored as given by (27). Thus Reference database consist a set $\{M_k\}$ of models. Each model M_k is defined by set of Gabor feature vectors $\{V_j\}$ extracted from feature points of model images. During storage process, each V_j is added to the reference database with a link to the model k for which it has been computed. So the reference database is table of couples (V_j, k).

$$V_{i,k} = \{x_k, y_k, R_{i,j}(x_k, y_k); j = 1, ...,16\} \qquad (27)$$

Here x_k, y_k = spatial co-ordinates of kth interest point and $R_{i,j}(x_k, y_k)$is j^{th} Gabor filter response at (x_k, y_k). To match test image, set of Gabor feature vectors $\{V_l\}$ are extracted from detected feature points on the test image. These vectors are compared with each of the vector V_j in reference database for similarity by using squared Euclidian distance metric given by equation (15). The most similar V_j for each V_l is identified and vote is given to the corresponding model. Then votes received by each model are summed and this sum is stored in the vector T (k). The model received more votes is considered as best match to the test image and is represented by the model $M_{\hat{k}}$ for which $\hat{k} = argmax_k T(k)$.It works on the assumption that if image similar to test image is stored in reference database, local features on the test image will be matched to the corresponding local features found on similar model images, while non-matching features on test image will be randomly spread over all the database images. As a result, the correct model image corresponding to test image will probably get more votes than the other model images, leading to a correct recognition.

3.3.5 Classifier 2-experimental results and analysis

The experiments are conducted to determine recognition rates obtained for illumination, pose and expression variations and results are represented graphically in Fig. 16. These experiments are performed with different number of feature points i.e. 50, 75 and 100 with the intention to determine optimum number of feature points required to achieve good recognition rate. It shows drastic improvement in performance. The recognition rates are 100% for pose and expression variations while the recognition rate for illumination variation is 78%. Actually recognition rates for pose and expression variations are same for 50, 75 and 100 feature points but comparatively on the basis of recognition rates achieved for illumination variations, recognition rates achieved with 75 feature points are excellent. It confirms that optimum number of feature points required to get good recognition rate with Classifier2 are 75. It also highlights the fact that to get good recognition rate fine tuned combination of feature point detector, feature extractor and classifier is very important.

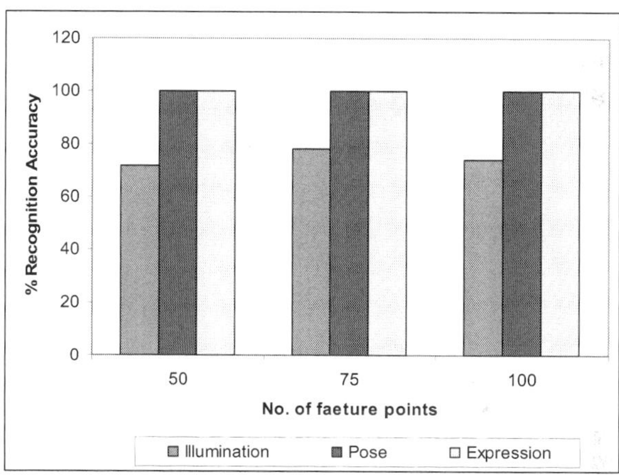

Fig. 16. Recognition rates obtained with Algorithm 3- Classifier 2

4. Performance analysis of proposed algorithms

The comparison of performances of proposed algorithms, as described in sections 3.1 to 3.3, is given in this section. Out of four variations of Algorithm 1, the performance achieved with use of illumination normalization as a pre-processing step to baseline algorithm is better with COS distance metric. This variation is referred as LFPCAIN i.e. local feature based PCA approach with illumination normalization as preprocessing step. The performance of Algorithm 2 was tested by using 10, 20 and 30 feature points with different distance metrics. It is observed that recognition rate obtained with 30 feature points and L1-norm distance metric is best. This variation is referred as LFPCA30 i.e. local feature based PCA approach with 30 feature points. The Algorithm 3 was implemented with Classifier1 and Classifier2. For Classifier1, performance obtained with 125 feature points and COS distance metric is best. This variation is referred as LFPCA125 i.e. local feature based PCA approach with 125 feature points. Similarly in case of Classifier2, recognition rate obtained with 75 feature points is best. This variation is referred as

LFVM75 i.e. local feature based voting mechanism approach with 75 feature points. The comparison of recognition rates achieved with above mentioned methods is carried out to select the most suitable algorithm for face recognition application. Moreover, the recognition rates reported in (Hwang at el., 2004) are also used for comparison because they reported recognition rates on Asian face database using holistic PCA approach for same image variations. The comparison of this approach with proposed algorithms will be helpful to check the effectiveness of the local feature based methods for face recognition application. This approach is referred as HPCA i.e. holistic feature based approach. The Fig. 17, 18, 19 and 20 shows this comparison for variations in illumination, pose, expression and average recognition rate respectively.

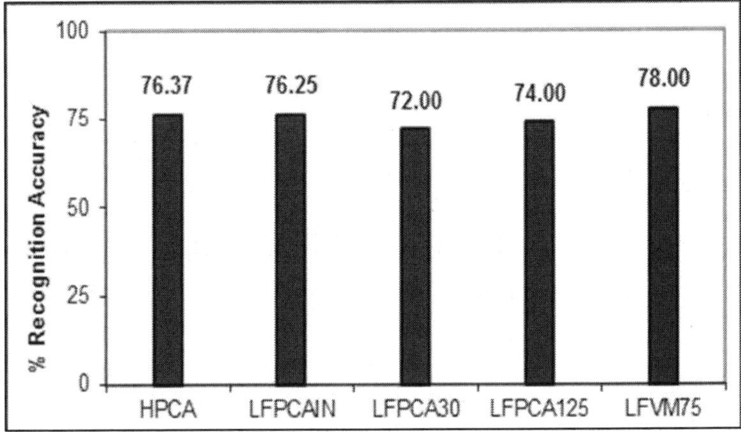

Fig. 17. Recognition rates comparison for illumination variation

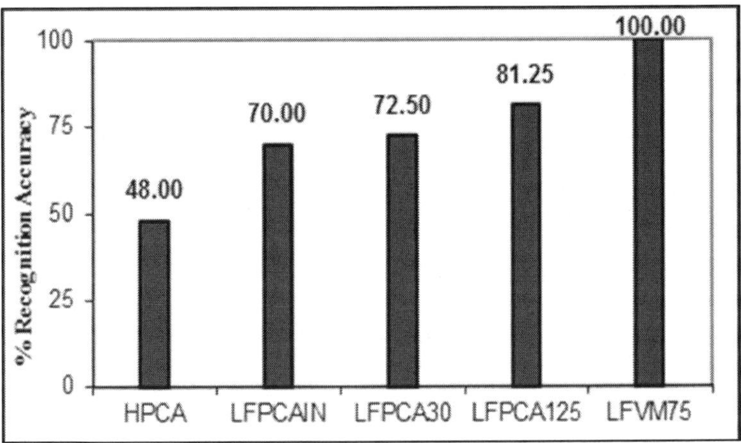

Fig. 18. Recognition rates comparison for pose variation

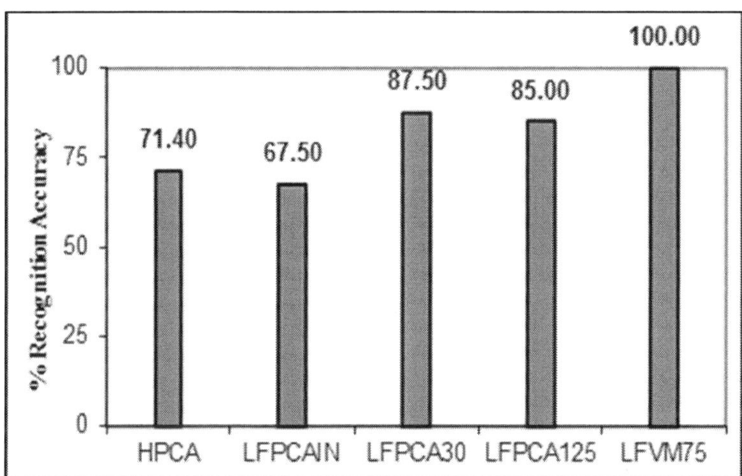

Fig. 19. Recognition rates comparison for expression variation

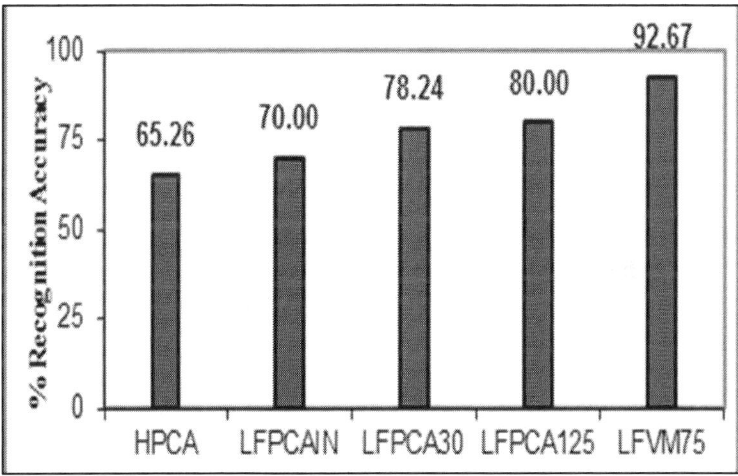

Fig. 20. Comparison of average recognition rates

It confirms that the local feature based algorithms are best suitable for face recognition applications because performances of all proposed local feature based algorithms are better than HPCA approach. Moreover, comparison also shows a continuous rise in recognition rate because each algorithm is proposed with the intention to overcome the limitations of previous algorithm. The maximum average recognition rate of 92.67% is reported by LFVM75 approach, and it reveals the fact that excellent recognition rate can be obtained by using invariant local feature detectors, invariant local feature descriptors and voting based classifier. The LFPCAIN approach uses Harris detector as feature point detector but Harris detector is not invariant to scale changes, and it results in lower recognition rate for pose and expression variations. This limitation of LFPCAIN approach is overcome by LFPCA30 approach with use of scale invariant feature point detector for detection of feature points. It results in increased recognition accuracy for pose and the expression variations but number of feature points detected is very less. In addition, most of the points represent same image structure and contribution of other important image structures is not taken into consideration while representing face image. It affects the discrimination ability of the classifier and hence recognition rate. These limitations are overcome by LFPCA125 approach. It used Harris-Laplace detector as a feature point detector and is truly invariant detector to most of the image transformations, and it results in increased recognition rate for all image variations. However, use of PCA for dimensionality reduction results in global feature vector and it nullifies the benefits of the local feature based methods. To avoid this, LFVM75 approach does classification of each local feature independently and results of individual classifiers are combined to get a final decision. It is achieved with voting mechanism, and it results in 100% recognition accuracy against pose and expression variations. The recognition accuracy against illumination variations is also increased considerably. The success rate achieved by LFVM75 approach highlights the fact that proper combination of a feature detector, feature descriptor and classifier is very much important to develop the highly efficient automatic face recognition system. The comparison of feature vector dimensionality of proposed local feature based methods with holistic method is given in Table 3. It shows that increased recognition rates are achieved with fewer numbers of feature points so that dimensionality of feature vectors gets drastically reduced. It further reduces the storage requirement, database size and execution time as well.

Approach	HPCA	LFPCAIN	LFPCA30	LFPCA125	LFVM75
Number of feature points	Whole image	14	30	125	75
Feature vector size	10304×1	224×1	480×1	2000×1	1200×1

Table 3. Comparison of feature vector dimensionality

5. Conclusion

The promising capability of the local feature based method for AFR is presented by taking advantage of recent developments in local feature detection and feature extraction techniques. The important issues addressed by proposed systems are: 1) robustness of the local feature based approach to pose, illumination and expression variations, 2) identification of optimum number of facial feature points required for face description and 3) requirement of fine tuned combination of feature detector, feature descriptor and classifier. The proposed algorithms works on color face images: after having localized the face, it determines and selects important fiducial facial points, and describes them by application of bank of Gabor filters. Finally classification is done with nearest neighbor classifier or voting based classifier. The experiments were carried out on KFDB and the experimental results confirms the superiority of the approach for face recognition. Nevertheless, most interesting point required to be consider is that the reported performance is obtained at reduced computation cost, storage requirement and computation time. All these advantages are very important for development of a practicable face recognition system.

6. References

Abate, F. Michele, N. Daniel, R. & Sabatino, G. (2007). 2D and 3D face recognition: A survey. Pattern Recognition Letters, Vol. 28, pp: 1885–1906.

Bartlett, M. Javier,M. Sejnowski, R. &Terrence, J. (2002). Face recognition by independent component analysis. *IEEE Transactions on Neural Networks*. Vol.13, No.6, pp: 1450–1464.

Belhumeur, P. Hespanha, J. & Kriegman, D. (1997). Eigenfaces vs. fisherfaces: Using class specific linear projection. *PAMI*, Vol.19, No. 7, pp: 711–720.

Beveridge, R. Bolme, D. Teixeira, M. & Draper, B. (2004). The CSU Face Identification Evaluation System. *Journal of Machine Vision and Applications*. Vol. 169, No. 2, pp: 128-138.

Ersi, E. & Zelek,J. (2006) Local Feature Matching For Face Recognition. *In Proceedings of The 3rd Canadian Conference on Computer and Robot Vision*. Canada, 2006.

Friedman, J. Hastie, T. & Tibshirani, R. (2000). Additive logistic regression: Astatistical viewof boosting. *Annals of Statistics*. Vol.28, No.2, pp: 337–374.

Heisele, B. Ho, P. Wu, J. & Poggio, T. (2003) Face recognition: Component- based versus global approaches. *Computer Vision and image Understanding*. Vol. 91, No.1, pp: 6–12.

Ho, T. Hull J. & Srihari, S. (1994). Decision combination in multiple classifier systems. *IEEE Transaction on PAMI*. Vol.16, No. 1, pp: 66–75.

Islam,M. Sluzek,A.Lin,Z.& Joo M. (2005) Towards Invariant Interest Point Detection of an Object. *Machine Graphics & Vision International Journal* . Vol.14,No.3, pp: 259 - 283.

Kittler, J. Hatef, M. Duin, R. & Matas, J. (1998). On combining classifiers. *IEEE Transaction on PAMI*. Vol. 20, No. 3, pp: 226–239.

Kisku,D. Rattani,A. Erosso,E. &Tistarelli,M. (2007). Face Identification by SIFT-based Complete Graph Topology. *In Proceedings of IEEE Workshop on Automatic Identification Advanced Technologies* , Alghero, 2007.

Lowe,D. (1999). Object recognition from local scale-invariant features. In proceedings of 7th IEEE International conference on computer vision. Kerkyra, Greece.

Lowe, D. (2004). Distinctive Image Features from Scale-Invariant Keypoints. *International journal of computer vision*, Vol. 60, No.2, pp:91-110.

Luo,J. Yong, M, Takikawa,E. Lao,S. Kawade,M.& Lu,B. (2007) Person -Specific SIFT Features For Face Recognition. *In Proceedings of IEEE International Conference on Acoustics, Speech and Signal Processing,* Honolulu, Hawaii, U.S., 2007.

Mandal, B. Jiang, D. Kot, A.(2006). Multi-Scale Feature Extraction for Face Recognition. *In Proceedings of 1st IEEE Conference on Industrial Electronics and Applications.* Singapore, 2006.

Mikolajczyk, K. & Schmid, C. (2002). An Affine Invariant Interest Point Detector. *In Proceedings of the 7th European Conference on Computer Vision,* Copenhagen, Denmark, 2002.

Mikolajczyk,K. (2004). Scale & affine invariant interest point detectors. *Computer Vision.* Vol.60, No.1, pp: 63–86.

This book chapter introduces two methods for evaluating the degree of facial paralysis. The first type is the computer-based realization of traditional medical methods, for example the House-Brackmann(H-B) method, mainly using image processing and pattern recognition techniques. In order to assess the degree of movement in the different regions of the face, the patients are first asked to perform five separate facial expressions, which are raising eyebrows, closing eye, screwing up nose, drumming cheek and opening mouth. The basic idea is to compare the differences between key points or regions in the two half sides of a face. Techniques involved in this type of methods include face detection, salient point or region detection, edge detection, clustering and machine learning schemes. This type of methods might require user interaction with the software system.

The second type of methods aims to automatically evaluate the facial paralysis and provide evaluation results without user intervention. Same as the first type of methods, patients are also asked to perform facial motions instructed by doctors. Salient regions and eigen-based methods are used to measure the asymmetry between the two sides of face and compare the expression variations between the abnormal and normal sides. Support vector machines are employed to produce the degree of paralysis. Both methods are tested on voluntary clinic patients. The strength and weakness of both methods are also presented.

2. Estimating degrees of facial paralysis based on Harris corner detection

First we describe the first one that is the computer-based realization of traditional medical methods, mainly using image processing and pattern recognition techniques. Our main goal is to find several key facial feature points and use these points to obtain the differences of motions between the two halves of the patient's face. These points include eye corners, nose corners and mouth corners. We first change the images into gray ones and then apply smoothing filters to the facial images so that noises can be reduced. This is because the images are unavoidably influenced by noises which make it difficult to obtain correct result. There are two purposes of filtering: 1. smoothing the regions that are not in edge region; 2. protecting edge regions. The median filter is an effective method to wipe out noise in images. In the next step, we apply integration projection on images to divide them into an eye region, a nose region and a mouth region. In each region, we use the Smallest Univalue Segment Assimilating Nucleus (SUSAN) algorithm and Harris corner detectors to locate feature points. Finally, we decide the paralysis degree by the combination of different scores derived from these points by comparing the two halves of the faces.

2.1 Integration projection for region detection

The integration projection method is based on the projection of an image into different directions. Let the processed image be $G(x,y)$, the size of which is M×N. Then the function of integration projection is described as follows:

The horizontal integration projection:

$$H(x) = \sum_{1}^{N} G(x,y) \tag{1}$$

The vertical integration projection:

$$V(y) = \sum_{1}^{M} G(x,y) \tag{2}$$

The two projections can be used to decide different regions.

2.2 Edge detection

Our previous experiments have shown that if we direct the corner detector on image, we may not obtain all the points as we wish. Thus, we first extract the edge in the image, and then apply the Harris corner detector.

We choose SUSAN edge detector (SM & JM, 2007) to extract edges. The SUSAN operator has been widely implemented by using circle masks. The usual radius is 3 to 4 pixels, and the smallest mask considered is the traditional 3×3 mask. The 37 pixel circular mask is used in all feature detection experiments unless otherwise stated.

The mask is placed at each point in the image and, for each point, the brightness of each pixel within the mask is compared with that of the nucleus (the centre point).Originally a simple equation determined this comparison:

$$c(\vec{r},\vec{r}_0) = \begin{cases} 1 & \text{if } | I(\vec{r}) - I(\vec{r}_0) | \leq t \\ 0 & \text{if } | I(\vec{r}) - I(\vec{r}_0) | > t \end{cases} \tag{3}$$

where:

$\vec{r}_0$ is the position of the nucleus in the two dimensional image;

$\vec{r}$ is the position of any other point within the mask;

$I(\vec{r})$ is the brightness of any pixel;

t is the brightness difference threshold and c is the output of the comparison.

This comparison is done for each pixel within the mask, and a running total n of the outputs(c)is expressed as:

$$n(\vec{r}_0) = \sum_{\vec{r}} c(\vec{r},\vec{r}_0) \tag{4}$$

Next, n is compared with a fixed threshold g, which is set to $3\,n_{max}/4$, where n_{max} is the maximum value which n can take. The initial edge response is created by using the following rule:

$$R(\vec{r}_0) = \begin{cases} g - n(\vec{r}_0) & \text{if } n(\vec{r}_0) < g \\ 0 & \text{otherwise,} \end{cases} \tag{5}$$

where $R(\vec{r}_0)$ is the initial edge response.

The algorithm as described above can produce good result. However, a much more stable and sensible equation that can be used for choosing c is:

$$c(\vec{r},\vec{r}_0) = e^{-\left(\frac{I(\vec{r}) - I(\vec{r}_0)}{t}\right)^6} \tag{6}$$

2.3 Corner detection

We use Harris corner detector to detect corners. The Harris corner detector (C & M, 1988) is a popular interest point detector due to its strong invariance to rotation, scale, illumination variation and image noise. The Harris corner detector is based on the local auto-correlation of a signal, where the local auto-correlation function measures the local changes of the signal with patches shifted by a small amount in different directions. A discrete predecessor of the Harris detector was presented by Moravec. Here the discreteness refers to the shifting of the patches.

Given a shift $(\Delta x, \Delta y)$ and a point (x_i, y_i), the auto-correlation function is defined as:

$$c(x,y) = \sum_W [I(x_i, y_i) - I(x_i + \Delta x, y_i + \Delta y)]^2 \tag{7}$$

where I denotes the image function and (x_i, y_i) are the points in the W (Gaussian window) centered on (x, y).

2.4 Algorithms for locating feature points

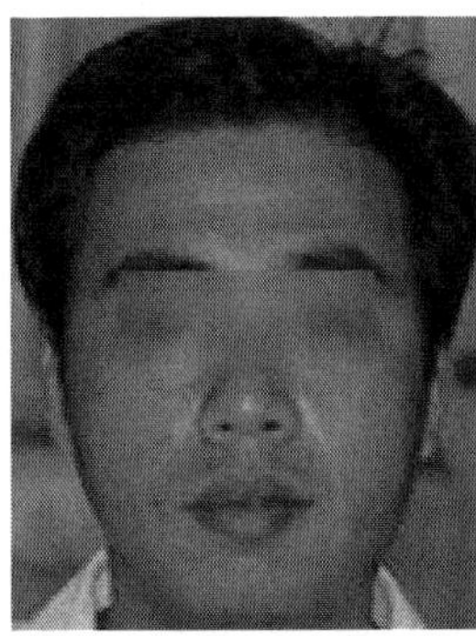

Fig. 1. An example image to be processed

2.4.1 Locating eyes regions and points

The location of eyes plays an important role in finding facial feature points. The following procedure can be used to locate eyes:

1. apply the Horizontal Integration Projection method on the image.
2. normalize the histogram of Integration Projection and find the y coordinate of the eyes according to minimum points of the histogram.
3. separate a region according to (2) and apply the Vertical Integration projection method to this region.
4. find two minimum points in the region and set them as the x coordinate of center of eyes.

After locating the eyes, we find the eyes region according to the center point. Then we apply Susan edge detector to extract edge and use the Harris corner detector to locate eyes corner points. There are some points we do not want; we choose left-most, right-most, top and bottom points.

Then we separate the eyebrow region based on the location of eyes. This is achieved by applying the Horizontal Integration Projection method on this region to find the y coordinate of the eyebrows, and then applying the Vertical Integration Projection method to find the x coordinate of the eyebrows.

Example results are shown in Fig. 2(a) and Fig. 2(b).

2.4.2 Locating nose region and points

Similar to locating eyes, the procedure for detecting the nose position is:

1. apply the Horizontal Integration Projection method to the region below the eye region;
2. find the first minimum point and set it as the y coordinate of the nose;
3. apply the Vertical Integration Projection to the region and set the height as [(y of nose)-(y of eyes)]*0.6;
4. find two minimum points and set them as the x coordinate of the hole of nose;
5. separate the nose region;
6. apply the SUSAN edge detection method on the region to extract edges and use the Harris corner detector.

We choose the left-most and right-most points.

Example results are shown in Fig. 2(c).

2.4.3 Locating the mouth region and points

Similar to methods introduced in previous sections, we first apply integration projection to the region below the nose and set the first minimum point as y of the mouth. According to this, we can find the mouth region. We use SUSAN method to extract edges and by using the Harris method we can find mouth corners and the middle line of the mouth. We choose the left-most, right-most and bottom points. The results are shown in Fig. 2(d).

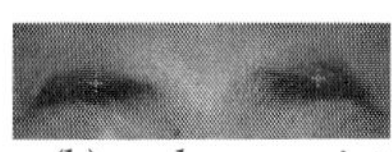

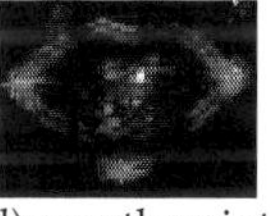

(a) eyes points   (b) eyebrow points   (c) nose points   (d) mouth points

Fig. 2. Results of locating feature points

2.5 The grading scheme

We capture facial images of patients while they perform expressions. Fig. 3 shows facial feature points we need. The following expressions are required and the corresponding distances are measured:

1. closing eyes: the distance of $S_0 I_0$ is calculated.
2. raising nose: the distance of $M_c L$ is calculated.
3. raising eyebrows: the distance of $S_0 I_0$ is calculated.
4. plumping cheek: the distance of $MMid$ is calculated.
5. opening mouth: the distance of $MMid$ is calculated.

In order to avoid the limitation of subjective decision, Burres presents an objective decision system (Burres & Fisch, 1986), namely linear measure index (B-FLMI), based on the research into calculating distances between certain points on human face. This system presents a method for recovery of face through measuring the percentage of distance (PD) of certain points. Although it can produce an objective evaluation of facial nerve, it is time consuming. In contrast, we apply face recognition techniques to evaluate facial condition.

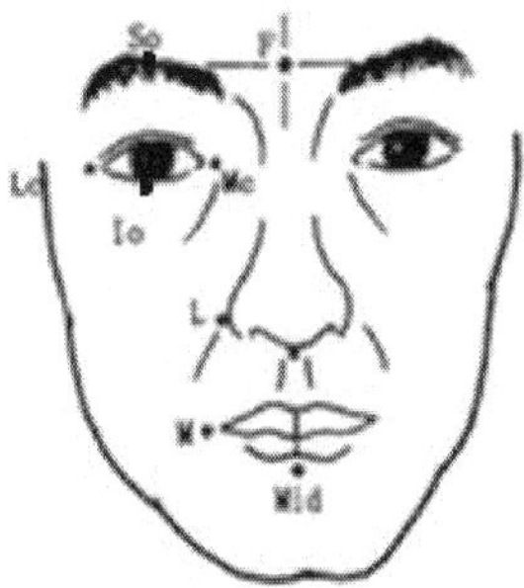

Fig. 3. Facial feature points (Junyu et al., 2008)

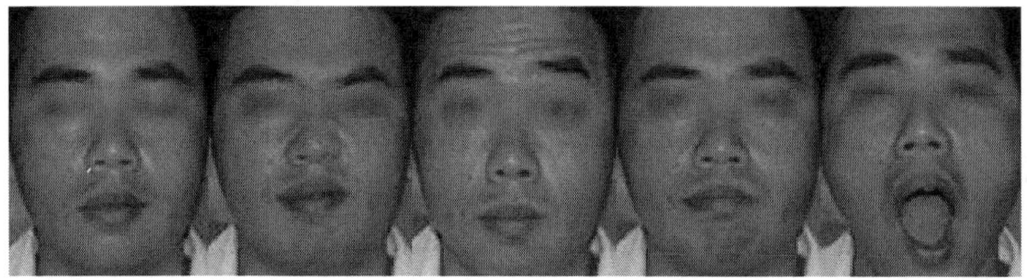

(a) close eyes   (b) raise nose   (c) raise eyebrow   (d) plump cheek   (e) open mouth

Fig. 4. Facial expressions made by a patient

The indices include:
1. two distance classes, i.e. D_1 indicates the measured distances between designated points of the healthy half of face and d_1 represents the distances between designated points on the sick half .
2. displacement percentage, i.e.

$$PD = d_1 \, / \, D_1 \, , if \, D_1 > d_1$$
$$PD = D_1 \, / \, d_1 \, , if \, D_1 < d_1 \tag{8}$$

3. FNI_1~FNI_5, which are indices of facial nerve function and denote the PD value of closing eyes, raising nose, raising eyebrow, plumping cheek, opening mouth.
4. the whole face nerve index, which is expressed as

$$TFNI = (sum \ of \ each \ FNI) \, / \, (number \ of \ indices) \tag{9}$$

5. the percentage of face nerve motion function, which is defined by

$$TPr = (unhealthy \ TFNI) \, / \, (healthy \ TFNI) \tag{10}$$

This system divides motions mentioned above into regions as follows: forehead, eyes, nose and mouth. The global evaluation method can also be used for locating regions.

The establishment of two indices, TFNI and TPr, is based on the overlay ratio of diagnose of facial paralysis. TPr is the ratio of TFNI measured twice.

Based on the formula:

$$T\,Pr = TFNI_2 \,/\, TFNI_1, TFNI = PD'/\,PD \tag{11}$$

We can obtain:

$$T\,Pr = (PD_1\,/\,PD_2) \times (PD_2'/\,PD_1') \tag{12}$$

PD1/PD2 is the ratio of two measurements of the healthy parts. This ratio reduces the error caused by two measurements. Because patients go to see the doctor only after they are affected by facial paralysis, we normally cannot get healthy TFNI. Thus, we can only employ unhealthy TFNI. The result will be more precise if both the two indices are considered.

The following rules are used to produce the final conclusion:

1.   if the value of TFNI is above 0.80, we can decide that the patient may recover after 1 month.
2.   if TPr is above 0.90, there is more assurance.
3.   if TPFI is 0.60~0.70 and TPr is larger than 0.75, the patient will recover in one year.
4.   if TPr is 0.80~0.85, they will recover in 2~3 months.

If TFNI is less than 0.40 and TPr is less than 0.50, the patient's face nerve is in bad condition and it should be treated early.

2.6 Experimental results

The experiments were carried out in a hospital. We ask 100 patients to perform certain facial expression and use the method introduced in the previous sections to evaluate the condition of patients. All images in our experiments were of frontal-viewed human faces and were warped to a standard size (200*250). The results are well consistent with the diagnosis based on a group of doctor's decision. The accuracy is above 95%. Table. 1 shows 10 example evaluation results. The final score is a weighted average of individual evaluation results.

	1	2	3	4	5	6	7	8	9	10
FNI1	0.75	0.67	0.84	0.78	0.84	0.76	0.76	0.90	0.95	0.65
FNI2	0.83	0.53	0.61	0.50	0.74	0.72	0.91	0.85	0.85	0.70
FNI3	0.75	0.41	0.83	0.89	0.90	0.63	0.43	0.74	0.75	0.64
FNI4	0.56	0.74	0.72	0.50	0.85	0.55	0.74	0.72	0.37	0.53
FNI5	0.95	0.88	0.75	0.59	0.91	0.92	0.83	0.64	0.50	0.74
TFNI	0.77	0.65	0.75	0.65	0.85	0.72	0.73	0.77	0.68	0.65

Table 1. Examples of grading results. Each column shows the evaluation result for each facial expression.

3. Estimating degrees of facial paralysis based on salient point detection

The key points introduced in the previous section can be seen as salient points, which are important for human visual system to capture key characteristics of an image. This section proposed another method for locating facial key points based on salient point detection.

In order to detect salient points quickly and accurately, we introduce a method based on wavelet transform. We first determine a set of key points based on salient point detection(Q et al., 2001), and then apply the K-MEANS clustering(K et al., 1998) algorithm to these key points and classify them into 6 categories. Finally, we calculate certain distances to estimate the state of facial paralysis.

3.1 Salient point detection

We apply a wavelet-based method for saliency detection to find the salient points which will include the key points we concern. The key points we concern include the two corners of the mouth, the topmost points of the two eyebrows, the internal and external corners of the eyes, the bottommost points of the eyes and the two points on the nosewing.

The wavelet representation of an image provides information about the variations in the image at different scales. We study the image at three scales 2^j, j= -1, -2, -3. At each scale, the image is decomposed into four sub-images. We use symbols LL, LH, HL and HH to represent approximate coefficients, horizontal details, vertical details and diagonal details respectively. In this paper, we denote the wavelet detail image as $W_2^j f$. We know from which signal points each wavelet coefficient at the scale 2^j is computed and we also calculate the coefficients at the scale 2^{j+1} at which the resolution is higher. There is a set of coefficients at the scale 2^{j+1} computed with the same points as a coefficient $W_2^j f(n)$ at the scale 2^j. The set of coefficients is denoted as $C\left(W_2^j f(n)\right)$ and we call it the children of the coefficient $W_2^j f(n)$. Their relationship is as follows:

$$C\left(W_{2^j}f(n)\right)=\left(w_{2^{j-1}}f(\kappa),2n\leq\kappa\leq 2n+2p-1\right),0\leq n\leq 2^j N \tag{13}$$

where p is the wavelet regularity and N is the length of the signal $2^{-j}p$. A formula that can compute salient values to extract salient points is as follows:

$$saliency=\sum_{k=1}^{-j}|C^{(k)}(W_{2^j}f(n))| \tag{14}$$

$$0\leq n\leq 2^j N,-\log_2 N\leq j\leq -1$$

We use the improved salient point detector based on wavelet transform instead of the above:

$$saliency=\sum_{k=1}^{-j}|w(k)C^{(k)}(W_{2^j}f(n))| \tag{15}$$

$$0 \leq n \leq 2^j N, -\log_2 N \leq j \leq -1$$

Where $w(k)$ is the weight of the maximum wavelet coefficients at different scales. $w(k)$ is calculated according to the following set of expressions:

$$\mu_\kappa = \frac{1}{S} \sum_{z=1}^{s} |W_{2^k} f(z)| \tag{16}$$

$$\sigma_\kappa = \frac{1}{S} \sum_{z=1}^{s} ([W_{2^k} f(z) - \mu_k]^2)^{\frac{1}{2}} \tag{17}$$

$$w(k) = \frac{1}{\sigma_k} \tag{18}$$

Where: S is the number of the set of maximum wavelet coefficients at k level:

$$0 \leq z \leq s$$

$|w_2^\kappa f(z)|$ is one of the elements of wavelet decomposition in the maximum coefficients.

A problem will appear when the patient's image contains closed eyes or mostly closed eyes. In this case, too many irrespective points can be found because of a great number of tiny wrinkles. Thus, the Log operator(D & E, 1980) is applied to find edges of eyes. Next, we choose the SUSAN edge detector to extract edges. When edges are extracted, the points that are not on the edges are discarded from the set of salient points. The remaining set of salient points is mostly points about facial features and we denote it as S.

3.2 K-MEANS clustering

Salient points S detected as described in the above section gather in the regions of eyebrows, eyes, nose, mouth and the contour of the face. In order to find the 14 key points in the facial features separately, the salient points need to be classified into six categories. We apply the K-MEANS clustering algorithm to S and classify them into 6 categories.

The main idea of K-MEANS is to define K centroids, one for each cluster. The steps are summarized as follows:

1. Select K points among the objects that are being clustered; these K points represent initial group centroids.
2. Assign each object to a group that has the closest centroid.
3. When all objects have been assigned, replace the K centroids with the new ones.
4. Repeat steps 2 and 3 until all the centroids do not change their positions any longer. The objects are separated into K groups finally.

3.3 Key point detection

We find the 14 key points on the edges of facial features respectively. The face model is shown as Figure 5:

We detect these key points among the salient points set S found in the previous section according to the edges detected through the SUSAN edge detection algorithm. The procedures for finding the topmost points of the two eyebrows are summarized as follows:

Valentine, T., & Bruce, V. (1986a). Recognizing familiar faces: The role of distinctiveness and familiarity. *Canadian Journal of Psychology, 40,* 300-305.

Valentine, T., & Bruce, V. (1986b). The effect of race, inversion and encoding activity upon face recognition. *Acta Psychologica, 61,* 259-273.

Valentine, T., & Bruce, V. (1986c). The effects of distinctiveness in recognising and classifying faces. *Perception, 15,* 525-535.

Valentine, T., & Bruce, V. (1988). Mental rotation of faces. *Memory and Cognition, 16,* 556-566.

Valentine, T., Chiroro, P., & Dixon, R. (1995). An account of the own-race bias and the contact hypothesis based on a 'face space' model of face recognition. In T. Valentine, (Ed.), *Cognitive and computational aspects of face recognition* (pp. 69-94). London: Routledge.

Valentine, T., & Endo, M. (1992). Towards an exemplar model of face processing: The effects of race and distinctiveness. *The Quarterly Journal of Experimental Psychology, 44A,* 671-703.

Valentine, T., & Ferrara, A. (1991). Typicality in categorization, recognition and identification: Evidence from face recognition. *British Journal of Psychology, 82,* 87-102.

Wickham, L. H. V., Morris, P. E., & Fritz, C. O. (2000). Facial distinctiveness: Its measurement, distribution and influence on immediate and delayed recognition. *British Journal of Psychology, 91,* 99-123.

Wright, D. B., Boyd, C. E., & Tredoux, C. G. (2003). Inter-racial contact and the own-race bias for face recognition in South Africa and England. *Applied Cognitive Psychology, 17,* 365-373.

Yin, R. K. (1969). Looking at upside-down faces. *Journal of Experimental Psychology, 81,* 141-145.

Yin, R. K. (1978). Face perception: A review of experiments with infants, normal adults, and brain-injured persons. In R. Held, H. W. Leibovitz, & H. L. Teuber (Eds.), *Handbook of sensory physiology,* Vol. 8: Perception (pp. 593-608). New York: Springer Verlag.

Part 3

Facial Image Database Development: Recognition Evaluation and Security Algorithms

7

A Face Image Database for Evaluating Out-of-Focus Blur

Qi Han, Qiong Li and Xiamu Niu
Harbin Institute of Technology
China

1. Introduction

Face recognition is one of the most popular research fields of computer vision and machine learning(Tores (2004); Zhao et al. (2003)). Along with investigation of face recognition algorithms and systems, many face image databases have been collected(Gross (2005)). Face databases are important for the advancement of the research field. Because of the nonrigidity and complex 3D structure of face, many factors influence the performance of face detection and recognition algorithms such as pose, expression, age, brightness, contrast, noise, blur and etc. Some early face databases gathered under strictly controlled environment(Belhumeur et al. (1997); Samaria & Harter (1994); Turk & Pentland (1991)) only allow slight expression variation. To investigate the relationships between algorithms' performance and the above factors, more face databases with larger scale and various characters were built in the past years(Bailly-Bailliere et al. (2003); Flynn et al. (2003); Gao et al. (2008); Georghiades et al. (2001); Hallinan (1995); Phillips et al. (2000); Sim et al. (2003)). For instance, The "CAS-PEAL", "FERET", "CMU PIE", and "Yale B" databases include various poses(Gao et al. (2008); Georghiades et al. (2001); Phillips et al. (2000); Sim et al. (2003)); The "Harvard RL", "CMU PIE" and "Yale B" databases involve more than 40 different conditions in illumination(Georghiades et al. (2001); Hallinan (1995); Sim et al. (2003)); And the "BANCA", and "ND HID" databases contain over 10 times gathering(Bailly-Bailliere et al. (2003); Flynn et al. (2003)). These databases help researchers to evaluate and improve their algorithms about face detection, recognition, and other purposes.

Blur is not the most important but still a notable factor affecting the performance of a biometric system(Fronthaler et al. (2006); Zamani et al. (2007)). The main reasons leading blur consist in out-of-focus of camera and motion of object, and the out-of-focus blur is more significant in the application environment of face recognition(Eskicioglu & Fisher (1995); Kim et al. (1998); Tanaka et al. (2007); Yitzhaky & Kopeika (1996)). To investigate the influence of blur on a face recognition system, a face image database with different conditions of clarity and efficient blur evaluating algorithms are needed. This chapter introduces a new face database built for the purpose of blur evaluation. The application environments of face recognition are analyzed firstly, then a image gathering scheme is designed. Two typical gathering facilities are used and the focus status are divided into 11 steps. Further, the blur assessment algorithms are summarized and the comparison between them is raised on the various-clarity database. The result of the comparison may give some advice on the selection of blur assessment algorithms and onwards help controlling the quality of the face recognition system.

The rest of this chapter is organized as follow: section 2 introduces the gathering scheme of the database and part of the reason. Section 3 describes the content of the database. Section 4 summarizes the blur assessment algorithms and raises test and comparison of them. The results are also shown in this section. Finally, the conclusion and future works are given in section 5.

2. The acquiring scheme of database

Most of the blur of digital image is caused by out-of-focus of camera or motion of objects. In the environments of face recognition system, the motion of face is not so fast, and a faster shutter may eliminate the motion blur in this case. Hence, the blur of face image is mostly caused by the out-of-focus of camera. The purpose of the new database is to help evaluating the blur assessment algorithms used in face recognition systems and the effect of the blur image on face recognition algorithms.

Around the topic of the database, an acquiring scheme is designed. The characters of the acquiring equipments are shown in table 1.

Equipment	PC camera	Professional camera
Number of pixels	$1,300,000$	$10,200,000$
Focus mode	manually	manually
Focus states	11	11

Table 1. Characters of acquiring equipments

28 volunteers were invited to contribute. The focus states are divided into 11 step include 10 out-of-focus states and 1 correct focused state. The expression is not restricted. Wearing glasses is allowed but will be gathered twice with glasses and without glasses. So the two equipments is expected to gather 682 frontal facial images in total.

3. The contents of database

The contents of the database are described in table 2. The database contains two parts of face images gathered from two typical facilities – a PC camera (Part I) and a digital single-lens reflex (DSLR) camera (Part II). Images in part I usually come with the face recognition applications in PC, mobile phone, ineternet authentication, and etc. While images in part II appear more in face detection, face retrieval and some other applications.

Figure 1 and 2 show some example images in the blur database. Figure 1 show images in part I and figure 2 show which in part II. 11 images of each faces are grouped into one troop. The correct focused image in part I is no.6, and that in part II is no.4. The shown samples are selected from the 11 images of each group(No.1,3,5,6,9,11 from part I, No.1,2,3,5,7,9 from part II).

	Part I	Part II
Individuals	28	28
Faces	31	31
With glasses	3	3
Male	11	11
Female	17	17
Race	Oriental	Oriental
Pose	Frontal	Frontal
Correct focus	1 image	1 image
Out of focus	10 images	10 images
Correct focused	No.6	No.4
Image size	320×240	2896×1936

Table 2. Overview of the blur face image databases

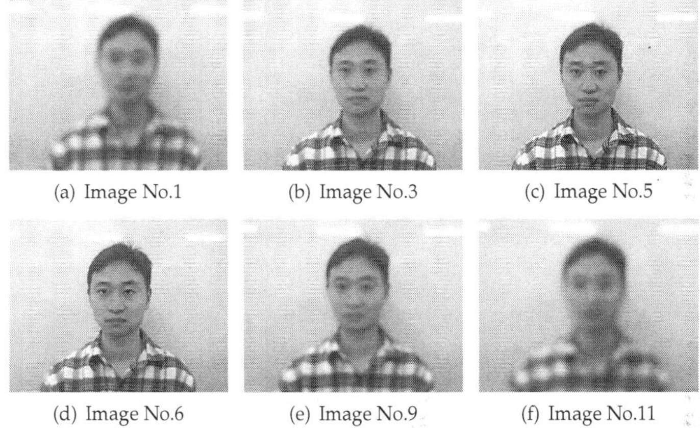

(a) Image No.1   (b) Image No.3   (c) Image No.5

(d) Image No.6   (e) Image No.9   (f) Image No.11

Fig. 1. Images acquired by PC camera (Fig.1(d) is the correct focused image)

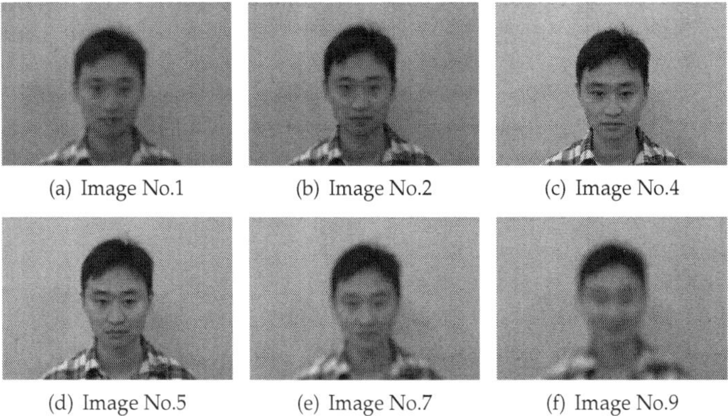

(a) Image No.1   (b) Image No.2   (c) Image No.4

(d) Image No.5   (e) Image No.7   (f) Image No.9

Fig. 2. Images acquired by DSLR camera (Fig.6(c) is the correct focused image)

4. The evaluation on blur assessment algorithms

Based on the database aiming on the image character of out-of-focus blur, a comprehensive evaluation of blur assessment algorithms is raised. The more credible benchmarking database, the result may be more universal – at least in the application fields related with face image.

4.1 The blur assessment algorithms

There are a great deal of blur assessment algorithms in literatures(Kim & Paik (1998); Li (2004); Maoyong et al. (2001); Subbarao et al. (1993)). Typical algorithms are summarized as follow (Suppose $f(x,y)$ is the grey scale value of pixel (x,y) of the image, N_x, N_y are the size of the image, and s is the clarity score.):

1. Variation of grey scale based algorithms:

   (alg-1) Variance of grey scale:

$$\bar{g} = \frac{1}{N_x \times N_y} \sum_{x=1}^{N_x} \sum_{y=1}^{N_y} f(x,y)$$

$$s = \frac{1}{N_x \times N_y} \sum_{x=1}^{N_x} \sum_{y=1}^{N_y} (f(x,y) - \bar{g})^2 \tag{1}$$

   (alg-2) Grey scale threshold. Define the average grey scale of a image as u. $f_H(x,y)$ means the grey scale value of all the C_H pixels satisfying $f(x,y) > (1+W)u$, and $f_L(x,y)$ means those of C_L pixels satisfying $f(x,y) < (1+W)u$. Then the clarity score is computed as:

$$\begin{cases} H = \sum_{x=1}^{N_x} \sum_{y=1}^{N_y} f_H(x,y)/C_H \\ L = \sum_{x=1}^{N_x} \sum_{y=1}^{N_y} f_L(x,y)/C_L \end{cases} \tag{2}$$

$$s = (H - L)/(H + L)$$

2. Gradient based algorithms:

   (alg-3) Sum of modulus of grey scale difference:

$$\Delta_x f(x,y) = f(x+1,y) - f(x,y)$$
$$\Delta_y f(x,y) = f(x,y+1) - f(x,y)$$
$$s = \sum_{x=1}^{N_x-1} \sum_{y=1}^{N_y-1} \{|\Delta_x f(x,y)| - |\Delta_y f(x,y)|\} \tag{3}$$

   (alg-4) Brenner function:

$$s = \sum_{x=1}^{N_x-2} \sum_{y=1}^{N_y} (f(x+2,y) - f(x,y))^2 \tag{4}$$

(alg-5) Square plane sum modulus difference:

$$s = \sum_{x=1}^{N_x-1} \sum_{y=1}^{N_y-1} (\Delta_x^2 + \Delta_y^2) \tag{5}$$

(alg-6) Sum of Roberts gradient:

$$s = \sum_{x=1}^{N_x-1} \sum_{y=1}^{N_y-1} \{|f(x,y) - f(x+1,y+1)| + |f(x+1,y) - f(x,y+1)|\} \tag{6}$$

(alg-7) Sum of Laplace gradient I:

$$\nabla f(x,y) = [f(x+1,y) + f(x-1,y) + f(x,y+1) + f(x,y-1)] - 4f(x,y)$$

$$s = \sum_{x=2}^{N_x-1} \sum_{y=2}^{N_y-1} |\nabla f(x,y)| \tag{7}$$

(alg-8) Sum of Laplace gradient II:

$$\nabla f(x,y) = [f(x+1,y) + f(x-1,y) + f(x,y+1) + f(x,y-1) + f(x+1,y-1) + f(x-1,y+1) + f(x+1,y-1) + f(x-1,y-1)] - 8f(x,y)$$

$$s = \sum_{x=2}^{N_x-1} \sum_{y=2}^{N_y-1} |\nabla f(x,y)| \tag{8}$$

(alg-9) Tenengrad function, define $f_x(x,y) = f(x,y) * K_x$ and $f_y(x,y) = f(x,y) * K_y$, where:

$$K_x = \begin{bmatrix} 0 & -1 & 0 \\ 0 & 2 & 0 \\ 0 & -1 & 0 \end{bmatrix}, \quad K_y = \begin{bmatrix} 0 & 0 & 0 \\ -1 & 2 & -1 \\ 0 & 0 & 0 \end{bmatrix} \tag{9}$$

Then:

$$s = \sqrt{f_x^2(x,y) + f_y^2(x,y)} \tag{10}$$

3. (alg-10) Grey scale entropy based algorithm, define $p(g)$ as the probability of the grey scale value g satisfies $g \in [0, G]$. Then:

$$s = -\sum_{g=0}^{G} p(g) \log p(g) \tag{11}$$

4. (alg-11) Fourier-Transform based algorithm:

$$F(u,v) = \sum_{x=1}^{N_x} \sum_{x=1}^{N_y} f(x,y) e^{[-j2\pi(xu/N_x + yv/N_y)]}$$

$$s = \left[\mathrm{Re}\left(\frac{F(u,v)}{\sum_{x=1}^{N_x}\sum_{y=1}^{N_y} f(x,y)} \right) \right]^2 + \left[\mathrm{Im}\left(\frac{F(u,v)}{\sum_{x=1}^{N_x}\sum_{y=1}^{N_y} f(x,y)} \right) \right]^2 \tag{12}$$

5. (alg-12) Wavelet-Transform based algorithm. Suppose A is the vector of decompose coefficients, the image size is $l \times l$, then:

$$s = \frac{1}{l^2-1} \left[\sum_{i=(l/2^m)^2}^{l^2-1} A[i]^2 \right] \tag{13}$$

6. (alg-13) Median filtering based algorithm. Define F' is the 3×3 median filtered result of image F. $D = |F - F'|$, then:

$$s = \sum_x \sum_y D(x,y) \tag{14}$$

Alg-1 to alg-13 are the most frequently used algorithms in literatures which cover the spatial domain and frequency domain methods. The evaluation over them aims to investigate their performance on face images. The references will be the clarity information recorded at gathering of the database. The guideline to evaluate an algorithm is correctness, susceptiveness and unimodality of the curve on the testing image database.

4.2 The evaluation on the database

To evaluate the performance of the blur assessment algorithms effectively, an evaluation scheme is designed as follow:

1. Implement a blur assessment algorithm A_i;

2. Compute the clarity scores of each image in each group, and get $31 \times 11 \times 2$ scores of the ith algorithm: $(s_{1,i}^I, s_{2,i}^I, \cdots, s_{11,i}^I), \cdots, (s_{1,i}^{II}, s_{2,i}^{II}, \cdots, s_{11,i}^{II})$;

3. Compute the average scores of each group in each part, and get 2 score sequences of each part of the database: $(s_1^I, s_2^I, \cdots, s_{11}^I)$ and $(s_1^{II}, s_2^{II}, \cdots, s_{11}^{II})$;

4. Go to step 1, repeat the process until all algorithms get their scores;

5. Plot these scores and analysis the result.

Because the image size of part II is 2896×1936 which is much bigger than that in part I (320×240). Another data set named part III is acquired via sampling from image in part II. The image size of part III is 362×242 which is close to part I. Some interesting results will be shown in the next section.

4.3 The results and analysis

The results of the evaluation are shown in figure 3 to figure 5. The algorithm-9 exhibits the best performance in part I and part III of database, while the algorithm-12 shows the stablest

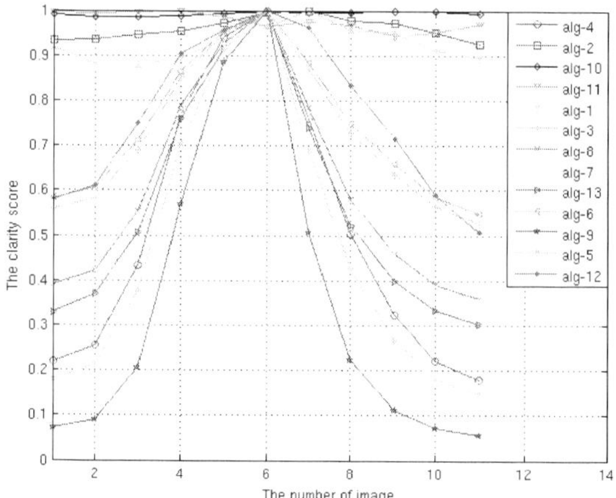

Fig. 3. The evaluating curves on part I

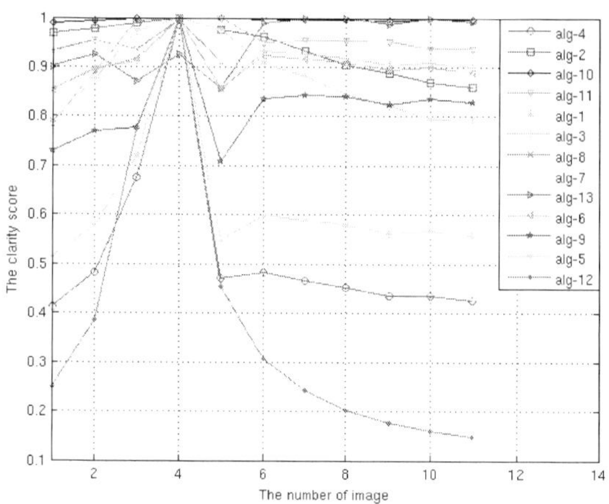

Fig. 4. The evaluating curves on part II

9

Face Recognition in Human: The Roles of Featural and Configurational Processing

Na Young Shin, Joon Hwan Jang and Jun Soo Kwon
Seoul National University
Republic of Korea

1. Introduction

During the last few decades, face perception has emerged as a prevailing issue in social research. Face recognition is a fundamental and crucial skill for communicating and understanding in human society. Fortunately, most adults are able to recognize faces to identify a particular face and to discriminate among faces at a glance, begging questions of the nature of the mechanisms that underlie such face recognition. It has been established that the processing involved in face recognition likely differs qualitatively from that involved in recognizing other objects. Indeed, responses to faces are more affected by inversion than are those to non-face objects. When faces are presented upside down, it is much harder to identify them accurately. Configurational properties are disrupted by presenting visual objects upside down or by laterally offsetting the top and bottom halves of objects, and greater disruption has been found when those objects are faces than when they are other types of objects (Maurer et al., 2002). Clinical studies have provided additional evidence of the special nature of face processing. Individuals with prosopagnosia experience difficulties with discriminating among human faces. They are able to perceive a face as face, but are unable to distinguish among different persons (Banich, 2004). Their deficit is specific to faces and derives neither from problems with visual perception nor from memory impairment. Neuroimaging studies have also indicated that the neural correlates involved in face recognition are distinct from those involved in the recognition of other objects.

Face processing can be divided into two types: configurational and featural (Maurer et al., 2007). Configurational processing refers to perceptions of the internal relationships among features. This approach contrasts with featural, analytic, piecemeal, or parts-based processing, which refers to perceptions of the shapes of individual features. The relative contributions of the two types of processing to face recognition and the interaction between them remain controversial. Although researchers have proposed different hypotheses about the mechanisms by which faces are processed on the basis of experimental findings, this issue is unresolved. In the context of the remarkable progress in brain imaging technology, recent studies have investigated the neural correlates of featural and configurational face processing, offering biological evidence related to behavioral phenomena. Consistent with these findings, this chapter addresses how humans recognize faces by reviewing the relevant findings from several research areas. In particular, the chapter focuses on the contributions of configurational and featural processing to face recognition. Based on behavioral and biological evidence, we will discuss how these two types of facial information are processed. For this purpose, we will discuss both aberrant and healthy approaches to recognizing faces, including psychiatric disorders other than prosopagnosia that are characterized by problems with recognizing faces. For example, patients with schizophrenia who suffer from psychotic symptoms such as hallucinations and delusions have shown impairments in their ability to perceive faces (Shin et al., 2008). Observations of individuals who suffer from impaired face recognition can provide important clues to the ways in which faces are processed.

2. Healthy processes underlying face recognition

2.1 Configurational and featural processing

Human faces share basic individual features including eyes, noses, and mouths as well as consistencies in the arrangement of these features (i.e., eyes above the nose and mouth below the nose). These common basic relationships among facial parts is known as a first-order configurational relationship (Diamond & Carey, 1986). First-order information is important for face detection (i.e., recognition of a stimulus as a face) (Kanwisher et al., 1998; Moscovitch et al., 1997). Even newborn infants have visual preferences for face or face-like stimuli that have first-order relationships (Johnson et al., 1991; Mondloch et al., 1999). On the other hand, the shapes of the features and the spatial distances between the features differ among individuals. Thus, to identify a particular person's face accurately, information about both the facial features and the spatial relationships among features must be encoded. The spatial distances among facial parts are referred to second-order configurational information, which is crucial for face identification and differentiation among faces (Diamond & Carey, 1986). Sensitivity to first-order relationships is important for face detection, whereas sensitivity to second-order relationships is crucial for the identification of particular individuals. According to developmental studies, configurational processing is available later in life (Brace et al., 2001; Carey & Diamond, 1977, 1994; Tanaka et al., 1998). Although several researchers have argued that even newborn infants were able to encode configurational information (Simion et al., 2007), access to second-order information seems to be unavailable until 4 years of age (Pellicano & Rhodes, 2003; Pellicano et al., 2006). Previous findings have suggested that young children recognize faces in ways that differ qualitatively from the ways in which adults recognize faces.

2.2 Measures of face recognition

Various manipulations of faces have been employed to elucidate the mechanisms underlying face recognition. In 1969, Yin compared the abilities of healthy subjects to recognize face and non-face objects presented in upright and inverted orientations (Yin, 1969). According to that study, the recognition of inverted faces was significantly more disrupted than that of inverted non-face objects such as houses and airplanes. Indeed, discrimination accuracy was reduced and reaction time was increased when faces were presented in an inverted position (Bartlett & Searcy, 1993). Inverting stimuli rendered objects more difficult to recognize, but the disruption was greater in response to faces than to other objects. This phenomenon, which has been termed the "inversion effect," has provided evidence that faces are distinct from other objects and that configurational information plays an important role in recognizing faces. Other frequently used manipulations of facial information have involved modifications of faces themselves (Leder & Bruce, 1998). As shown as Figure 1, featural information can be altered by modifying the shapes of specific features (a). Similarly, second-order configurational information can be manipulated by changing the distances between specific features but maintaining the shapes of features as unchanged (b). Other alterations in facial information can involve the gradual blurring of faces (Fig. 1c) (Sergent, 1986). The blurred faces degraded featural information more severely than configurational information. When blurred faces were inverted, both featural and configurational information were disrupted, resulting in severe impairments in recognition (Collishaw & Hole, 2000).

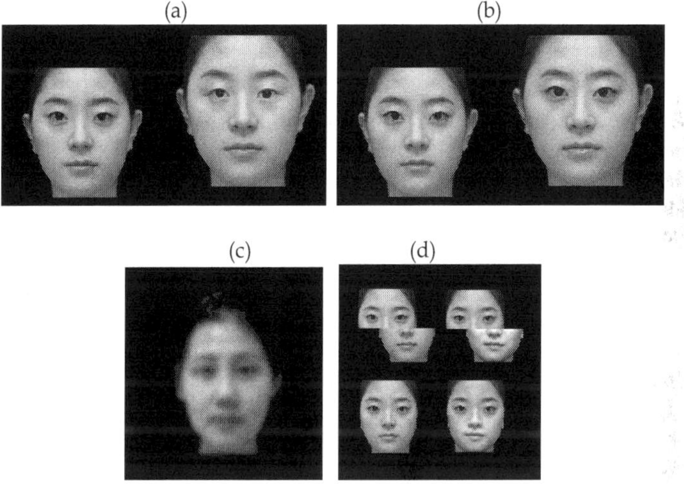

Fig. 1. Examples of the manipulation of facial information. (a) an alteration of featural information by replacing eyes with other female of the same race. (b) an alteration of configurational information by modifying distance between eyes. (c) a blurred face (d) composite faces

Another frequently employed technique is a composite face (Fig. 1d), in which the top half of one face is paired with the bottom half of another face and presented as a whole face or is offset laterally. When adults were asked to discriminate the top halves of a pair of faces, their discrimination performance was slower and less accurate under the whole-face condition than under the offset condition, indicating the holistic processing of face recognition (Young et al., 1987). This phenomenon is known as the "composite-face effect." Various techniques have facilitated progress in research on face recognition. Measures have been modified, and new techniques have been created to examine how featural and configurational information affected face recognition. In the next section, we will focus on the role of featural and configurational processing in face recognition, on the relationship between two types of processing, and finally on whether the two types of information rest on differentiated or shared biological mechanisms.

2.4 Biological evidence

Although a substantial body of evidence has shown how faces are processed behaviorally, these data have been limited to confirming the contributions of featural and configurational information to face recognition. Recent neuroimaging studies have used various techniques such as event-related potentials (ERPs), magnetoencephalography (MEG), and functional magnetic resonance imaging (fMRI) to provide evidence about the brain correlates of face perception. More recently, researchers have attempted to find the distinct neural mechanisms underlying each featural and configurational process. Biological evidence may help us to understand the way in which faces are processed, even though the neural mechanisms underpinning face recognition have not been fully elucidated due to the small number of studies.

2.4.1 Evidence from neurophysiology

ERP studies investigating face processing have reported the involvement of various electrophysiological components including P100 (P1), N170, and P200 (P2), primarily in the posterior cortex (Bentin & Deouell, 2000; Boutsen et al., 2006; Pesciarelli et al., in press; Rossion et al., 2000). In particular, the N170 component, with a negative peak at about 170 ms after stimulus onset, appeared to reflect face-specific processing. The amplitude of N170 is greater in response to faces than to objects (Boutsen et al., 2006) and is sensitive to the inversion effect (Bentin et al., 1996; Eimer, 2000; Rossion et al., 1999). Inversion of faces induces increased and delayed activity in N170 of the right hemisphere, indicating that this component may be involved with the configurational processing related to face recognition (Rossion et al., 1999). However, the aspects of face processing to which N170 is sensitive remain uncertain. Scott and Nelson (2006) observed that activity in the right hemisphere N170 was greater for configurational processing, whereas activity in the left hemisphere N170 was greater for featural processing. Mercure et al. (2008) examined ERPs using a similar task but did not find that featural and configurational alterations affected N170. Instead, that study found that the amplitude of P2 was greater in response to configurational modification. Although the particular ERP components that modulated the two types of facial information remain uncertain, limited neurophysiological evidence has implied that featural and configurational processing are likely mediated by differential neural correlates.

2.4.2 Evidence from functional neuroimaging

Many previous studies have detected a face-specific brain area, the so-called "face area." The fusiform face area (FFA), which is located in the region of the occipito–temporal cortex, has shown increased activity during the viewing of faces (Downing et al., 2006; Grill-Spector et al., 2006; J. V. Haxby et al., 2000; J.V. Haxby et al., 1994; Kanwisher et al., 1997). However, the neural activity in this brain region did not seem to selectively respond to specific types of face processing (Aguirre et al., 1999; R. Epstein et al., 2006; J. V. Haxby et al., 1999; Kanwisher et al., 1998; Mazard et al., 2006; Schiltz & Rossion, 2006). Yovel and Kanwisher (2004) investigated neural activity while subjects discriminated whether pairs of faces were the same or different. Stimuli were modified in terms of either the shapes of facial features or the distances between features. The central finding was that FFA activity did not differ under featural and configurational conditions, indicating the absence of face-processing activity specific to the FFA. Indeed, *many neuroimaging* studies have sought to associate FFA activity with an inversion effect, but most could not find increased activity in this area (J. V. Haxby et al., 1999; Kanwisher et al., 1998; Schiltz & Rossion, 2006). In this context, the brain regions specific to each type of face processing remain unidentified. Maurer et al. (2007) investigated the neural mechanism underpinning featural and configurational processing using featurally or configurationally altered face stimuli. They reported that the right fusiform area, which is adjacent to the FFA, exhibited more activity in response to spacing than to features (Fig. 2). In addition to the right fusiform area, multiple regions in the right frontal cortex also showed increased activity during configurational processing, whereas left prefrontal activity increased during featural processing. These findings suggest that the neural correlates involved in the processing of second-order information are likely to differ from those involved in featural processing. Another similar study from Switzerland supported this notion by showing dissociated neural pathways associated with featural and configurational processing during face recognition (Lobmaier et al., 2008). Although no consensus on what brain regions are associated with each type of face processing has been reached thus far, speculation favoring separate neural networks for featural and configurational processing appears plausible.

3. Aberrant face-recognition processing

Close examination of patients who suffer from impaired face recognition should provide important insights into the mechanisms underlying face processing. Similar to studies focusing on healthy face processing, recent studies examining abnormal face recognition have attempted to identify the aspects of face processing that are impaired in disorders of face recognition. Interestingly, visual agnosia, which refers to the inability to recognize visual stimuli, is domain-specific. Indeed, damage to various brain areas caused various types of agnosia. For example, topographical agnosia, which results from damage to the parahippocampal area, is characterized by impairment in scene recognition despite intact object recognition, (R. Epstein et al., 2001). Prosopagnosia is a kind of face-specific agnosia in which patients experience difficulty in indentifying the faces even in the absence of other kinds of visual agnosia. Some patients have suffered from deficits after damage to specific brain areas such as the occipito–temporal cortex (acquired prosopagnosia), whereas others have suffered from these deficits in the absence of neurological damage (developmental or congenital prosopagnosia). Due to the specificity of deficits in face recognition, the mechanism underlying prosopagnosia has been extensively studied in research addressing face recognition. Patients with psychiatric disorders such as schizophrenia also experience problems with face recognition, but their deficits derive primarily from neurodevelopmental alterations in the brain rather than from invasive brain damage (Cornblatt et al., 2003). Patients with schizophrenia have shown dysfunction in various cognitive domains including working memory, executive functioning (Antonova et al., 2004), and social perception (Marwick & Hall, 2008). Difficulties with the perception of social objects and the interpretation of social contexts have been identified as especially critical contributors to the outcomes of the illness, although the question of whether social dysfunction in schizophrenia is associated with other sorts of cognitive deficits remains debatable.

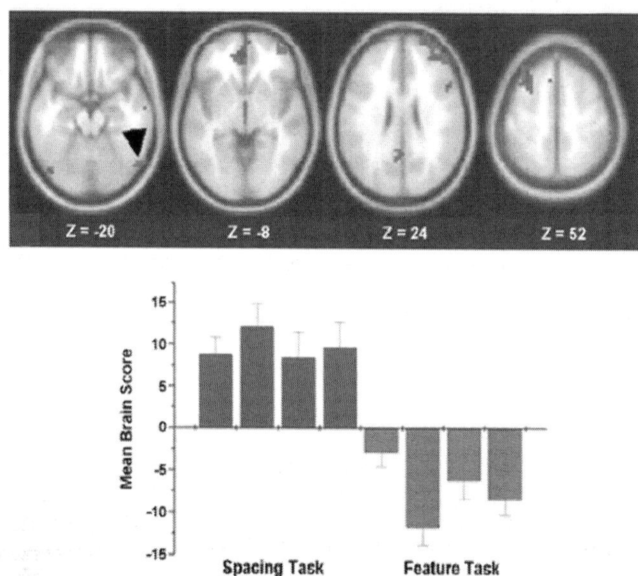

Fig. 2. Neural correlates of face recognition. Brain regions (upper panel) and the pattern of activity (lower panel) involved with the featural (blue) and configurational processing (red). Adapted from Maurer et al. (2007)

3.1 Prosopagnosia

Prosopagnosia is a rare deficit characterized by impaired face identification. Patients with this neurological disorder experience difficulties with face recognition but function in an intact manner in tasks involving the visual recognition of non-face objects. Many studies have reported findings from single cases (Ariel & Sadeh, 1996; Bentin et al., 1999; Busigny & Rossion, in press; de Gelder & Rouw, 2000; Duchaine, 2000; Duchaine et al., 2003; McConachie, 1976; Saumier et al., 2001; Steeves et al., 2006; Wilkinson et al., 2009). Although several studies have compared the performances of groups, individual differences, even within the patient group, have been prominent, especially in the case of developmental prosopagnosia (Le Grand et al., 2006). The core question raised by these studies involves the nature of the face-recognition impairment in prosopagnosia. One influential early view held that these patients experienced difficulties with recognizing faces holistically (Levine & Calvanio, 1989). According to this assumption, patients failed to integrate featural information into a whole representation. This view appeared to be compelling for patients with acquired prosopagnosia who showed damage to the brain areas primarily linked to the occipito–temporal cortex. However, findings regarding developmental prosopagnosia have varied in that patients have shown individual differences on the same task due to the heterogeneity of this disorder. For example, of the eight patients with developmental prosopagnosia studied by Le Grand et al. (2006), seven showed normal abilities to the discriminate the top halves of faces under the misaligned condition; indeed, their performance under the misaligned condition was better than that under the aligned condition, indicating intact holistic processing. Additionally, two patients showed specific deficits in the discrimination either of featurally or of configurationally modified faces, whereas one patient showed abnormalities in the ability to process both types of facial information. Another case study compared two patients, one with prosopagnosia and the other with object agnosia, to examine interactions between featural and configurational processing (Rivest et al., 2009). The main finding of this study was that the patient with prosopagnosia showed impairment in processing featural and configurational facial information, whereas the patient with object agnosia exhibited deficits in only featural processing despite normal face-recognition ability. The authors noted that configurational processing is required for face recognition and that therefore featural processing cannot proceed without configurational processing. Taken together, and despite the remaining controversy about the nature of face processing, the deficits found in studies related to prosopagnosia have implicated differentiated mechanisms underlying configurational and featural processing as well as their interactions.

3.2 Schizophrenia

Schizophrenia is a neuropsychiatric disorder characterized by social dysfunction as well as abnormal mental processes such as hallucinations and delusions. Patients with schizophrenia have difficulty identifying social objects such as faces (Joshua & Rossell, 2009; Shin et al., 2008) and bodies (Takahashi et al., 2010), recognizing facial expressions (Aleman & Kahn, 2005; Doop & Park, 2009; Morris et al., 2009; Pinkham et al., 2007), and understanding the mental states of others (Brüne & Brüne-Cohrs, 2006; Chung et al., 2008; Corcoran et al., 1995; Pinkham et al., 2003). Recent studies have investigated the basic mechanisms underlying impaired face recognition in this disorder. Shin et al. (2008) compared patients with schizophrenia with healthy control subjects without psychiatric histories in their ability to discriminate modified faces. This study found that patients with schizophrenia were less accurate in discriminating faces that differed with respect to configurational or featural facial information, whereas their ability to recognize modified non-face objects such as chairs was normal. Interestingly, the impairment in the ability to recognize configurational information was much greater than that in the ability to discriminate featural information. Additionally, the inversion effect was reduced among those with schizophrenia compared with those in the control group, indicating disrupted configurational processing among those with this disorder (Fig. 3).

However, because both configurational and featural processing were abnormal in the patients in this study, the specific aspects of face processing that contributed to aberrant face recognition remain unclear. A recent study investigated the face-recognition abilities of individuals at risk for the development of schizophrenia (Kim et al., 2010). The results indicated that subjects at risk showed alterations only in their ability to discriminate configurational, not featural, information. This observation suggested the possibility that the impairments involved in configurational processing in the service of face recognition begin earlier than do those involved in featural processing and that featural processing gradually deteriorates prior to the onset of the illness. Another study from Australia reported similar findings in patients with schizophrenia (Joshua & Rossell, 2009). Patients with schizophrenia did not rely as heavily on configurational information as did control subjects, indicating less use of configurational processing. In this context, the difficulties with face recognition experienced by patients with schizophrenia can probably be attributed to impairment in configurational processing. Deficient configurational processing may force patients to rely on featural information to recognize faces, resulting in imperfect face recognition.

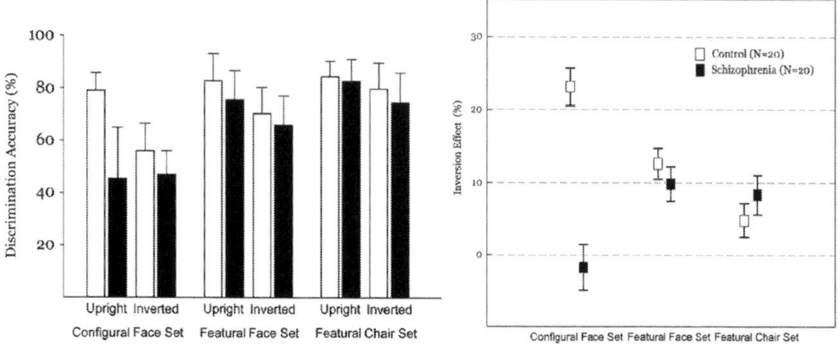

Fig. 3. Comparison of face discrimination performance between patients with schizophrenia and healthy controls. Adapted from Shin et al. (2008)

4. Conclusion

The ability to recognize faces is crucial for social communication and adaptation in human societies. Although several research approaches have sought to provide a clear answer to how and on what basis faces are recognized, this questions remain unanswered at this point. Relatively confirmatory long-standing evidence has suggested that face processing is distinct from the processing of non-face objects; this evidence has included behavioral phenomena such as the inversion effect, the existence of a face-specific disorder such as prosopagnosia, and neural correlates (e.g., the FFA) that have exhibited relative selectivity in their responses to faces. The first line of behavioral studies has provided various effective tasks or techniques to enable differentiation between featural and configurational processing, establishing a foundation for identifying the mechanisms underlying face recognition. Observations from behavioral studies have served as a basis for ideas and assumptions about how featural and configurational processing contribute to face recognition. Nonetheless, behavioral data do not consistently and clearly explain whether one type of processing plays a dominant role in face recognition or whether both types of facial processing interact or act independently. An extreme view has argued that holistic processing, in interaction with featural information, dominates face recognition. At the other extreme, arguments that featural information is processed independently and is critical for face recognition have been advanced. A neutral view holds that both featural and configurational data are important and that they interact in the accurate and efficient recognition of faces. According to limited recent evidence, the last assumption appears to be the most plausible. Some patients with prosopagnosia were unable to utilize configurational information, but others failed to recognize featural information, although all showed difficulties in the identification of faces. This evidence raises questions about whether people would fail to recognize faces if one type of process were disrupted. In other words, do both types of processing make essential contributions to accurate face recognition? Recent evidence has implicated the operation of separate neural mechanisms for featural and configurational processing. If featural and configurational processing interact during face recognition, it can be presumed that the two types of information, processed in separate brain regions, would be connected through neural networks that function in an interactive way. Future studies investigating neural connectivity will help our understanding of the nature of the interplay between featural and configurational face processing and will clarify how faces are processed. Indeed, studies conducted from within different domains — including neuropsychology, neurophysiology, neuroimaging, neurology, and psychiatry — should be synthesized. The data collected thus far are insufficient for determining the processes underlying face recognition. Future research using effective tasks is needed to elucidate the neuropsychological mechanisms and neural correlates involved in healthy and abnormal face processing.

5. Acknowledgment

This work was supported by WCU (World Class University) program through the Korea Science and Engineering Foundation funded by the Ministry of Education, Science and Technology (R31-2009-000-10089-0)

6. References

Aguirre, G. K., Singh, R., & D'Esposito, M. (1999). Stimulus Inversion and the Responses of Face and Object-Sensitive Cortical Areas. *Neuroreport*, Vol.10, No.1, 189-194, ISSN 0959-4965.

Aleman, A. & Kahn, R. (2005). Strange Feelings: Do Amygdala Abnormalities Dysregulate the Emotional Brain in Schizophrenia? *Progress in Neurobiology*, Vol.77, No.5, 283-298, ISSN 0301-0082.

Amishav, R. & Kimchi, R. (2010). Perceptual Integrality of Componential and Configural Information in Faces. *Psychonomic Bulletin & Review*, Vol.17, No.5, 743-748, ISSN 1069-9384.

Antonova, E., Sharma, T., Morris, R., & Kumari, V. (2004). The Relationship Between Brain Structure and Neurocognition in Schizophrenia: A Selective Review. *Schizophrenia Research*, Vol.70, No.2-3, 117-145, ISSN 0920-9964.

Ariel, R. & Sadeh, M. (1996). Congenital Visual Agnosia and Prosopagnosia in a Child: A Case Report. *Cortex*, Vol.32, No.2, 221-240, ISSN 0010-9452.

Banich, M. T. (2004). Face Recognition in Human, In: *Cognitive Neuroscience and Neuropsychology*, pp. 203-208, Houghton Mifflin Company, ISBN 0618122109, Boston.

Bartlett, J. C. & Searcy, J. (1993). Inversion and Configuration of Faces. *Cognitive Psychology*, Vol.25, No.3, 281-316, ISSN 0010-0285.

Bentin, S., Allison, T., Puce, A., Perez, E., & McCarthy, G. (1996). Electrophysiological Studies of Face Perception in Humans. *Journal of Cognitive Neuroscience*, Vol.8, No.6, 551-565, ISSN 1530-8898.

Bentin, S. & Deouell, L. Y. (2000). Structural Encoding and Identification in Face Processing: ERP Evidence for Separate Mechanisms. *Cognitive Neuropsychology*, Vol.17, No.1, 35-55, ISSN 0264-3294.

Bentin, S., Deouell, L. Y., & Soroker, N. (1999). Selective Visual Streaming in Face Recognition: Evidence from Developmental Prosopagnosia. *Neuroreport*, Vol.10, No.4, 823-827, ISSN 0959-4965

Lobmaier, J. S., Klaver, P., Loenneker, T., Martin, E., & Mast, F. W. (2008). Featural and Configural Face Processing Strategies: Evidence from a Functional Magnetic Resonance Imaging Study. *Neuroreport,* Vol.19, No.3, 287-291 ISSN 0959-4965.

Marwick, K. & Hall, J. (2008). Social Cognition in Schizophrenia: A Review of Face Processing. *British Medical Bulletin,* Vol.88, No.1, 43-58, ISSN 1471-8391.

Maurer, D., Grand, R. L., & Mondloch, C. J. (2002). The Many Faces of Configural Processing. *Trends in Cognitive Sciences,* Vol.6, No.6, 255-260, ISSN 1879-307X.

Maurer, D., O'Craven, K. M., Le Grand, R., Mondloch, C. J., Springer, M. V., Lewis, T. L., & Grady, C. L. (2007). Neural Correlates of Processing Facial Identity Based on Features Versus Their Spacing. *Neuropsychologia,* Vol.45, No.7, 1438-1451, ISSN 1873-3514.

Mazard, A., Schiltz, C., & Rossion, B. (2006). Recovery from Adaptation to Facial Identity Is Larger for Upright than Inverted Faces in the Human Occipito-temporal Cortex. *Neuropsychologia,* Vol.44, No.6, 912-922, ISSN 0028-3932

McConachie, H. R. (1976). Developmental Prosopagnosia. A Single Case Report. *Cortex,* Vol.12, No.1, 76-82, ISSN 0010-9452

Mercure, E., Dick, F., & Johnson, M. H. (2008). Featural and Configural Face Processing Differentially Modulate ERP Components. *Brain Research,* Vol.1239, 162-170, ISSN 0006-8993.

Mondloch, C. J., Lewis, T. L., Budreau, D. R., Maurer, D., Dannemiller, J. L., Stephens, B. R., & Kleiner-Gathercoal, K. A. (1999). Face Perception During Early Infancy. *Psychological Science,* Vol.10, No.5, 419-422, ISSN 0956-7976.

Morris, R. W., Weickert, C. S., & Loughland, C. (2009). Emotional Face Processing in Schizophrenia. *Current Opinion in Psychiatry,* Vol.22, No.2, 140-146, ISSN 0951-7367.

Moscovitch, M., Winocur, G., & Behrmann, M. (1997). What Is Special about Face Recognition? Nineteen Experiments on a Person with Visual Object Agnosia and Dyslexia But Normal Face Recognition. *Journal of Cognitive Neuroscience,* Vol.9, No.5, 555-604, ISSN 0898-929X.

Pellicano, E. & Rhodes, G. (2003). Holistic Processing of Faces in Preschool Children and Adults. *Psychological Science,* Vol.14, No.6, 618-622, ISSN 0956-7976.

Pellicano, E., Rhodes, G., & Peters, M. (2006). Are Preschoolers Sensitive to Configural Information in Faces? *Developmental Science,* Vol.9, No.3, 270-277, ISSN 1467-7687.

Pesciarelli, F., Sarlo, M., & Leo, I. (in press). The Time Course of Implicit Processing of Facial Features: An Event-Related Potential Study. *Neuropsychologia,* ISSN 0028-3932.

Pinkham, A. E., Penn, D. L., Perkins, D. O., Graham, K. A., & Siegel, M. (2007). Emotion Perception and Social Skill over the Course of Psychosis: A Comparison of Individuals "At-risk" for Psychosis and Individuals with Early and Chronic Schizophrenia Spectrum Illness. *Cognitive Neuropsychiatry,* Vol.12, No.3, 198 - 212, ISSN 1354-6805.

Pinkham, A. E., Penn, D. L., Perkins, D. O., & Lieberman, J. (2003). Implications for the Neural Basis of Social Cognition for the Study of Schizophrenia. *American Journal of Psychiatry,* Vol.160, No.5, 815-824, ISSN 0002-953X.

Rakover, S. S. & Teucher, B. (1997). Facial Inversion Effects: Parts and Whole Relationship. *Perception & Psychophysics,* Vol.59, No.5, 752-761, ISSN 0031-5117.

Rivest, J., Moscovitch, M., & Black, S. (2009). A Comparative Case Study of Face Recognition: The Contribution of Configural and Part-based Recognition Systems, and Their Interaction. *Neuropsychologia*, Vol.47, No.13, 2798-2811, ISSN 0028-3932.

Rossion, B., Delvenne, J. F., Debatisse, D., Goffaux, V., Bruyer, R., Crommelinck, M., & Guerit, J. M. (1999). Spatio-temporal Localization of the Face Inversion Effect: An Event-Related Potentials Study. *Biological Psychology*, Vol.50, No.3, 173-189, ISSN 0301-0511.

Rossion, B., Gauthier, I., Tarr, M. J., Despland, P., Bruyer, R., Linotte, S., & Crommelinck, M. (2000). The N170 Occipito-temporal Component is Delayed and Enhanced to Inverted Faces But Not to Inverted Objects: An Electrophysiological Account of Face-specific Processes in the Human Brain. *Neuroreport*, Vol.11, No.1, 69-74, ISSN 0959-4965.

Saumier, D., Arguin, M., & Lassonde, M. (2001). Prosopagnosia: A Case Study Involving Problems in Processing Configural Information. *Brain and Cognition*, Vol.46, No.1-2, 255-259, ISSN 0278-2626.

Schiltz, C. & Rossion, B. (2006). Faces are Represented Holistically in the Human Occipito-temporal Cortex. *NeuroImage*, Vol.32, No.3, 1385-1394, ISSN 1053-8119.

Scott, L. S. & Nelson, C. A. (2006). Featural and Configural Face Processing in Adults and Infants: A Behavioral and Electrophysiological Investigation. *Perception*, Vol.35, No.8, 1107-1128, ISSN 0301-0066.

Searcy, J. H. & Bartlett, J. C. (1996). Inversion and Processing of Component and Spatial-Relational Information in Faces. *Journal of Experimental Psychology: Human Perception and Performance*, Vol.22, No.4, 904-915, ISSN 1939-1277.

Sergent, J. (1986). Microgenesis of Face Perception In: *Aspects of face processing*, H. Ellis, M. Jeeves, F. Newcombe & A. Young (Eds.), pp. 17-33, Dordrecht, Kluwer.

Shin, Y. W., Na, M. H., Ha, T. H., Kang, D. H., Yoo, S. Y., & Kwon, J. S. (2008). Dysfunction in Configural Face Processing in Patients with Schizophrenia. *Schizophrenia Bulletin*, Vol.34, No.3, 538-543, ISSN 1745-1701.

Simion, F., Leo, I., Turati, C., Valenza, E., & Dalla Barba, B. (2007). How Face Specialization Emerges in the First Months of Life. *Progress in Brain Research*, Vol.164, 169-185, ISSN 0079-6123.

Steeves, J. K. E., Culham, J. C., Duchaine, B. C., Pratesi, C. C., Valyear, K. F., Schindler, I., Humphrey, G. K., Milner, A. D., & Goodale, M. A. (2006). The Fusiform Face Area Is Not Sufficient for Face Recognition: Evidence from a Patient with Dense Prosopagnosia and No Occipital Face Area. *Neuropsychologia*, Vol.44, No.4, 594-609, ISSN 0028-3932.

Takahashi, H., Kato, M., Sassa, T., Shibuya, T., Koeda, M., Yahata, N., Matsuura, M., Asai, K., Suhara, T., & Okubo, Y. (2010). Functional Deficits in the Extrastriate Body Area During Observation of Sports-Related Actions in Schizophrenia. *Schizophrenia Bulletin*, Vol.36, No.3, 642-647, ISSN 1745-1701

Tanaka, J. W. & Farah, M. J. (1993). Parts and Wholes in Face Recognition. *The Quarterly Journal of Experimental Psychology Section A*, Vol.46, No.2, 225-245, ISSN 0272-4987.

Tanaka, J. W., Kay, J. B., Grinnell, E., Stansfield, B., & Szechter, L. (1998). Face Recognition in Young Children: When the Whole is Greater than the Sum of Its Parts. *Visual Cognition*, Vol.5, No.4, 479-496, ISSN 1350-6285.

Tanaka, J. W. & Sengco, J. A. (1997). Features and Their Configuration in Face Recognition. *Memory and Cognition,* Vol.25, No.5, 583-592, ISSN 0090-502X.

Valentine, T. & Bruce, V. (1988). Mental Rotation of Faces. *Memory & Cognition,* Vol.16, No.6, 556-566, ISSN 0090-502X.

Wilkinson, D., Ko, P., Wiriadjaja, A., Kilduff, P., McGlinchey, R., & Milberg, W. (2009). Unilateral Damage to the Right Cerebral Hemisphere Disrupts the Apprehension of Whole Faces and Their Component Parts. *Neuropsychologia,* Vol.47, No.7, 1701-1711, ISSN 0028-3932.

Yin, R. K. (1969). Looking at Upside-down Faces. *Journal of Experimental Psychology,* Vol.81, No.1, 141-145, ISSN 1076-898X.

Young, A. W., Hellawell, D., & Hay, D. C. (1987). Configurational Information in Face Perception. *Perception,* Vol.16, No.6, 747-759, ISSN 0301-0066.

Yovel, G. & Kanwisher, N. (2004). Face Perception: Domain Specific, Not Process Specific. *Neuron,* Vol.44, No.5, 889-898, ISSN 0896-6273.

10

Psychiatric Disorders of Face Recognition

Chloé Wallach and Sadeq Haouzir
Centre Hospitalier du Rouvray
France

1. Introduction

Reports of cases of patients suffering from an impairment of the brain function of face recognition have appeared in the medical literature since 1923. In some instances the cause is a cerebral accident, others occur in the context of a psychiatric condition.

Those face recognition disorders associated with psychiatric diseases are called misidentification syndromes and may be less well known by clinicians.

There are several syndromes, all defined by the delusional belief that familiar people or even the patient himself have been replaced by doubles or sosies.

The first and most common disorder to have been described is the Capgras delusion named after French Professor Jean-Marie Joseph Capgras who, with his intern Jean Reboul-Lachaux, first described this "curious little syndrome"[1] as he named it (Capgras & Reboul-Lachaux, 1923).

1.1 Clinical interest of Capgras delusion

Clinical studies of this pathology are justified and valuable because it is a disease that is stable over time, that can last for years and that is similar between patients whatever the context.

Hence Capgras delusion seems to be a basic concept, a clinical entity that is found in several diseases, both of lesional (neurologic, iatrogenic, infectious…) or psychiatric etiology. This observation has given rise to numerous debates about whether Capgras delusion is a symptom or a syndrome, a controversy that we won't discuss in this chapter.

1.2 Psychopathological interest

Understanding the abnormality in Capgras delusion could help understand the physiology underlying the identification and recognition of individuals by the human brain.

In this chapter, we first clinically describe the Capgras delusion and other misidentification syndromes in their historic version. Then we examine the different explanatory models that have been reported in the scientific literature, considering psychodynamical hypotheses, neurocognitive and neuro-lesional theories and finally global models.

---

[1] In French "un curieux petit syndrome"

2. Clinical description of misidentification syndromes

2.1 Some epidemiological data

Several classifications of psychiatric diseases have been developed because psychiatry is mainly a clinical science. As Capgras delusion occurs in many diseases, no standard definition exists for this particular entity in the current international classifications such as in the Diagnostic and Statistical manual of Mental disorders (APA, 1994) or the International Classification of diseases (WHO, 2010).

Thus evaluating its frequency is challenging. Capgras delusion is believed to occur seldom (or stays unnoticed), but seems to be the most common of the misidentification syndromes known.

Its prevalence varies widely across studies. Huang et al. report a prevalence of 2.5% among patients admitted in the psychiatric unit of the Memorial Hospital of Chang Gung in Taiwan between October 1994 and November 1995 (Huang et al., 1999, as cited in Henriet et al., 2008) against 0.14% for Fischbain among patients admitted to the psychiatric emergency unit of the Jackson Memorial Hospital in Miami during the year 1983 (Fishbain, 1987, as cited in Henriet et al., 2008).

2.2 Historical description of Capgras delusion

French Professor Jean-Marie Joseph Capgras and his intern Jean Reboul-Lachaux presented the original case of Mrs M. to the Clinical Society of Mental Health in Paris in 1923. He first termed it "l'illusion des sosies" (Capgras & Reboul-Lachaux, 1923).

Mrs M., a 53 year old seamstress, was living in Paris with her husband and their 20 year old daughter. She was hospitalized in 1919 in the French psychiatric hospital Maison-Blanche after asking the Police to help her free the many people sequestrated in the basement of her house and throughout Paris. Professor Capgras reported how Mrs M. explained that she was the victim of a vast conspiracy of "sosies", real people being imprisoned underground while their doubles act badly.

"Her husband [...] also disappeared: a sosie took his place; she wanted to divorce this sosie; she drew up a complaint and requested a separation from the court. Her real husband was murdered and the "gentlemen" who come to visit her at the hospital are "sosies" of her husband; she counted at least eighty of them. [...] "If this person is my husband, she says, he is totally unrecognizable, he is transformed. I certify that this so-called husband that they are trying to foist on me in fact ceased to exist ten years ago".[2]

"To replace my stolen daughter, they always put another one who was in turn removed and immediately replaced ... Whenever they took away a child, they gave me another one who looked like her. I had over two thousand in five years [...]. Every day girls came to my home and every day they were taken away; I warned the Police Superintendent, saying that their parents had disappeared and that these girls had pricks to the face to remove all their ideas

---

[2] In French "Son mari [...] a également disparu : un sosie a pris sa place ; elle a voulu divorcer d'avec ce sosie ; elle a adressé une plainte et fait une demande de séparation au Palais. Son véritable mari a été assassiné et "les messieurs" qui viennent la voir sont des "sosies" de son mari ; elle en a compté au moins quatre-vingts. [...] Si cette personne est mon mari, il est plus que méconnaissable, c'est une personne métamorphosée. Je certifie que le prétendant mari que l'on cherche à m'insinuer pour le mien n'existe plus depuis dix ans. "

and that they were abused ... This coming and going of children at my house lasted from 1914 to 1918 without interruption."[3]

"But disappearances go well beyond the family of Mrs. M., extending to her household, to the whole world and especially to Paris. [...] All the people who are around Mrs M. every day at the hospital have their sosies. [...] The head of department has been replaced by sosies and when asked if she is certain, she stops and then, with conviction, exclaims "The doctors who come here with a cloak, you can't tell me there is only one: I know at least fifteen of them! ""[4]

The patient herself uses the word "sosie". The concept of the existence of doubles is the clinical particularity of this delusion for Capgras.

Capgrass and Reboul-Lachaux explained the process of face recognition as a struggle between two feelings caused by the visual stimulus: a sense of familiarity and a sense of strangeness, which he compared with the mixed feelings one has when confronted with someone one hasn't seen in a long time.

In the case of Mrs. M., the sensory recognition is associated with the feeling of strangeness, the sense of familiarity has disappeared. Capgras believed it didn't come from a sensory disorder but from a primary affective disorder with a secondary delusional interpretation or, as Capgras said "an emotional state first, then a habit, finally an automatic state of mind."[5]

2.3 Other misidentification syndromes are known
2.3.1 Fregoli delusion

The "syndrome d'illusion de Frégoli" was first described in 1927 by two French psychiatrists, Paul Courbon and Gustave Fail (Courbon & Fail, 1927, as cited in Henriet et al., 2008).

In this syndrome, the patient holds the delusion that different people who have no physical resemblance are in fact a single person who changes appearance or is in disguise, like the famous Italian actor Leopoldo Fregoli (1867-1936) who was renowned for his ability to make quick changes of appearance during his stage act.

In the original case, a 27 year old French woman, a servant, believed she was the victim of two actresses, Sarah Bernhardt and Robine, who had the capacity to take over the bodies of the people she met, to take her thoughts or to make her do specific acts. Her persecutors had

---

[3] "Pour me remplacer ma propre fille volée, on en mettait toujours une, à son tour enlevée et remplacée aussitôt… Au fur et à mesure qu'ils m'enlevaient une enfant, ils m'en donnaient une autre qui lui ressemblait. J'en ai eu plus de deux mille en cinq ans [...] Il venait journellement des fillettes chez moi qui journellement m'étaient enlevées ; j'ai prévenu le Commissaire de police du quartier Necker lui disant que leurs parents avaient disparu et que ces fillettes avaient des piqûres à la physionomie pour leur enlever toute idée et qu'elles étaient maltraitées… Ce va-et-vient d'enfants chez moi a duré de 1914 à 1918, sans discontinuer."

[4] "Mais les disparitions débordent largement le milieu familial de Mme M., pour s'étendre à sa maison, au monde entier et spécialement à Paris. [...] Tous les gens qui entourent journellement Mme M. à l'asile ont leurs sosies. [...] On a remplacé le chef de service par des sosies et comme on lui demande si elle en est bien certaine, elle s'arrête, puis, avec conviction, s'exclame "Les docteurs qui viennent ici avec les pèlerines, vous ne me direz pas qu'il n'y en a qu'un : j'en connais au moins quinze ! " "

[5] In French "un état affectif d'abord, une habitude, une tournure d'esprit ensuite"

the power of Fregoli and could even "fregolify" other people, meaning to put other people than themselves inside the bodies of relatives of the patient.

2.3.2 Intermetamorphosis or "syndrome d'intermétamorphose et de charme"

Soon after Capgras delusion and Fregoli syndrome, a case of "intermetamorphosis" was presented to the medical and psychological society meeting in Paris by Paul Courbon and Jean Tusques (Courbon & Tusques, 1932).

The main symptom is the belief that the body and soul of different people are incarnated in the body of a single person.

2.3.3 The syndrome of subjective doubles

In this more recently described pathology (Christodoulou, 1978, as cited in Henriet et al., 2008), the subject experiences the illusion that he or she has one or more doubles with the same physical appearance but different character traits, with each double leading a life of its own.

2.4 What misidentification syndromes have in common (Weinstein, 1994, as cited in Henriet, 2003)

A first common trait is the belief in duplication of people. Each patient suffering from one of these syndromes has the idea that multiple versions of people can exist at the same moment (but not at the same place).

This illusion of substitution comes from an agnosia of identification: the impersonator is physically identical (i.e. physically recognized) but psychologically different (the sense of familiarity that should accompany the visual recognition has disappeared).

The impersonator uses his resemblance with the real person to persecute the patient; he is always ill intentioned.

The person replaced isn't chosen at random. In most cases the person is emotionally related to the patient, by attraction or repulsion.

Finally, in every case, the fate of the « original » person seems quite unimportant: he or she may have disappeared, been kidnapped, confined, murdered… The explanations are often poor and evasive, given with little emotion.

2.5 Their differences according to the literature

To work on these syndromes, authors tried to classify them according to their differences, suggesting that the psychopathology processes could be different.

For Jacques Vié in 1930, all of the misidentification syndromes are a single disease that he calls "syndrome des sosies" and that can take two forms: a positive and a negative form. In the first category, the patient finds imaginary resemblances between people; Vié in this case describes the sosies as "positive", as in Fregoli delusion or intermetamorphosis. In the second category, the person denies the identity of his relative, discovering tiny differences between the "original" person and his sosie, creating a "negative" double. Capgras delusion or the syndrome of subjective doubles are examples of the negative form of syndrome des sosies (Vié, 1930).

Georgios Christodoulou in 1977 proposed the same kind of classification, distinguishing hypo-identification from hyper-identification syndromes (Christodoulou, 1977, as cited in Henriet, 2003). Some specific facial recognition tests could differentiate between these two sub-groups of patients suggesting that the facial recognition process is altered in different ways in the two groups (Walther et al., 2010).

Oyebode in 1996 identified patients who recognize familiar faces (Capgras), and patients who recognize unfamiliar faces (Frégoli). According to this author, this distinction could mean that these two syndromes come from two different anatomical lesions, considering that the recognition process for familiar faces would be located in the right temporal lobe whereas for unfamiliar faces the right parietal lobe would be implicated (Oyebode et al., 1996, as cited in Henriet, 2003).

2.6 These clinical entities are found in several pathologies

Capgras delusion can be associated with organic diseases like epilepsy, stroke, iatrogenic pathologies or infectious diseases. Capgras delusion seems to be mostly found coupled with psychiatric disorders, mainly paranoid schizophrenia, but also mood or schizoaffective disorders.

A case of isolated Capgras was described by Henriet et al. in 2006. A 59 year old woman believed her husband and daughter were replaced by evil sosies. The paraclinical test results (blood test, electroencephalogram, cerebral scan, single photon emission computed tomography, intellectual efficiency) were normal, showing no neurological disease. The psychiatric exam didn't reveal any schizophrenia, chronic hallucinatory psychosis, paranoid psychosis or mood disorder. She had a similar episode four years earlier and recovered without treatment at the time, keeping her social and professional position.

2.7 Differential diagnosis

The "recognitions" in Capgras delusion are different from false recognitions which are defined by the recognition of an unknown person. Patients with false recognitions perceive face similarities when there aren't any whereas patients with Capgras detect tiny details to justify their denial of the identity of the person.

Capgras is not a memory disorder because the patient doesn't have any trouble remembering the faces of the people whose identity he denies.

Capgras differs also from prosopagnosia. The latter is the inability to recognize faces of familiar people by sight (but the person can be recognized by his or her voice, glasses, mustache...), but is not accompanied by the mention of the existence of sosies or by persecutory delusional experiences.

The symptoms of paramnesia of reduplication look like Capgras delusion because the patient holds the delusional belief that a place or a person familiar to him has been duplicated, but there isn't any notion of substitution or imposture.

3. Explanatory models of face recognition

Three categories of models have been considered in the scientific literature. Psychodynamic theories inspired by psychoanalysis were initially preferred given the selective nature and the emotional value of the sosified person (most of the time a family member, or the patient's caregiver).

Neuro-lesional models have been developed starting from the 1960s with the objective of locating the face processing area in the human brain, using anatomical and functional neuro-imaging techniques.

More recently the development of cognitive neuropsychology offered a different approach based on models of the face processing function, trying to discover not the brain structure responsible for the dysfunction, but the cognitive operation deficiency.

3.1 Psychodynamic models

These models were mainly developed at the time of the first description in 1923, approximately when Sigmund Freud was elaborating his psychoanalytic theories, in particular in his book "The Uncanny" ("Das Unheimliche") where he discusses the concept of the "double" (Freud, 1919, as cited in Henriet, 2003).

The first theory is the hypothesis of depersonalization where the notion of sosie would be due to the projection by the patient of his own "Uncanny" on others. The patient finds it easier to believe that others have changed rather than himself. Hence the impression of "not being oneself" becomes the impression of others "not being themselves", having been replaced by sosies.

The most widely accepted psychodynamic theory currently is the hypothesis that Capgras delusion is a psychotic solution to the problem of ambivalence.

The definition of ambivalence in psychoanalysis is the fact of having simultaneously contradictory feelings toward a person, usually love and hate. The defense mechanism used to cope with these conflicting feelings depends on personality.

For patients suffering from Capgras delusion, the defense mechanism used to cope with the split between the feeling of hate and the feeling of love would be the idea of the existence of two persons: a bad one, the sosie, considered as an impostor and a persecutor, and a good one, the "original" person. This theory allows the patient to continue loving his or her relative while expressing his or her hate of the sosie without any feeling of guilt.

Capgras delusion is also believed to result from early relational disturbances, or a childhood trauma causing a loss of confidence in the reality of the objective world or even an attempt to overcome a poorly repressed Oedipius complex.

Jean-Marie Joseph Capgras' own etiological hypothesis is a primary affective disorder because of the simultaneous feelings of familiarity and strangeness. He explained that the belief in sosies is the intellectual conclusion of disturbed feelings.

3.2 Psychometrics

Neuropsychological tests are based on the concept of the human face as a specific recognition object. Thus the human face is seen as a geometric figure that changes with age, mood, health status, presence of accessories (glasses, make-up …) or expressed emotions.

Psychometric tests use match-to sample, discrimination or naming of human faces which differ in the viewing angle, the sex, the age, the expressed emotion, the pose, the features... For instance, the Benton Face Recognition Test (Benton & Van Allen, 1968 as cited in Vanier, 1991) evaluates face identification skills by matching pictures of non familiar faces presenting differences in the lighting or the viewing angle. The Bruyer and Schweich face recognition battery uses a famous faces discrimination task and identification subtests of features independent of the expression (Bruyer & Schweich, 1991). Familiarity can also be experimentally induced before the tests with repeated exposure to a face.

Neuropsychological models have been developed based on the test errors observed in Capgras delusion and prosopagnosia patients.

3.2.1 Bruce and Young's sequential model
Bruce and Young imagined a three step model of face recognition that progresses in a particular order (Bruce & Young, 1986, as cited in Ellis, 2004).

The first step is the encoding (i.e the conversion of the stimulus to information that can be stored in memory) of general physical characteristics such as age, sex or skin color and of physiognomic characteristics that are unique to this face.

The next step is the comparison of this information with the memory stock of familiar people (composed of different Face Recognition Units or FRU), producing or not the feeling of familiarity.

If the face is familiar, the final step consists of the stimulation by the FRU of the Person Identity Node (or PIN) containing the relevant semantic and biographical information.

In Capgras delusion, the third step would be disturbed resulting in a dysfunction of the access to the sosified person's PIN, the recognition of his face (steps 1 and 2) being preserved but not his identification. The familiar face activates the information related to the imaginary persecutor and not those of the real person.

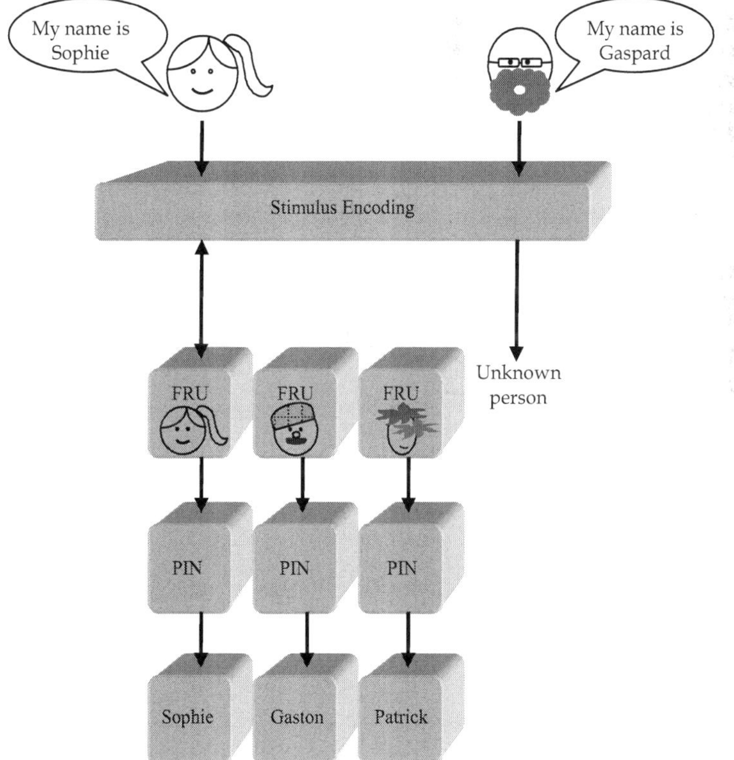

Fig. 1. A simplified version of Bruce & Young's sequential model. A familiar face activates the corresponding Face Recognition Unit (FRU), then the Personal Identity Node (PIN), finally the Name Retrieval Module (Bruce & Young, 1986, as cited in Ellis, 2004).

This sequential model is currently supplanted by a serial model which better accounts for Capgras delusion.

3.2.2 The two-route model of face recognition has become a widely accepted hypothesis

Bauer suggested another model, based on the observed emotional reactivity caused by a face in prosopagnosic patients (Bauer, 1984, 1986, as cited in Breen et al., 2000). He assumed that emotional reactivity could be measured by "skin conductance response" (which varies with the skin's sweating level), and that a change in this parameter would represent an unconscious recognition of the face. In prosopagnosia, a change in the patient's skin conductance response appears when he is confronted with a familiar face, but he isn't capable of consciously recognizing his relative. Bauer concluded that there are two parallel pathways, instead of one in the first model, connecting the visual cortex to the limbic system (an association of cerebral areas believed to support emotion, behavior, and memory skills).

The first is an overt ventral route via the inferior temporal lobe which makes it possible to recognize consciously and explicitly the identity of the observed face.

The second is the covert dorsal route going via the superior temporal sulcus and the inferior parietal lobule which is responsible for the affective and unconscious recognition of the face.

In a 1990 paper published in the British Journal of Psychiatry, psychologists Ellis and Young, considering Bauer's model, suggested that Capgras delusion could result from a dysfunction of the dorsal route with an intact ventral route (Ellis & Young, 1990, as cited in Henriet et al., 2008).

In the case of patients with Capgras delusion, the Ellis and Young hypothesis was confirmed with the observation of a deficit in emotional reactivity while the conscious awareness of recognition is preserved (Hirstein & Ramachandran, 1997). The patient physically recognizes his relative's face but doesn't have the affective confirmation of this recognition. Faced with this conflicting information, he calls upon rationalization and concludes that there must be a sosie of his relative. The authors emphasized the fact that the face recognition deficit in Capgras delusion is selective to the visual domain. Indeed some patients remain capable of recognizing their sosified relative by his voice.

Ellis and Young also hypothesized Capgras delusion could be the "mirror" of prosopagnosia. In Bauer's model, prosopagnosia would represent an interruption in the overt route, whereas Capgras delusion would result from an impairment of the covert pathway.

3.2.3 Breen's serial model

Breen et al. proposed in 2000 a bidirectional cognitive model of face processing based on Bauer's model. They state that there isn't any evidence supporting the theory of two anatomical regions responsible for face recognition. Thus they claim that the visual-limbic ventral route described by Bauer is the sole face processing area of the human brain.

They argue that within this area there are two functional pathways from the Face Recognition Unit, one leading to the related Personal Identity Node, the other to an "affective response to familiar stimuli" module. The two pathways are independent.

According to the authors, Capgras delusion would be the outcome of a lesion or a dysfunction in the access to the additional module, whereas prosopagnosia would be the result of a dysfunction in the FRU or in the access to the associated PIN.

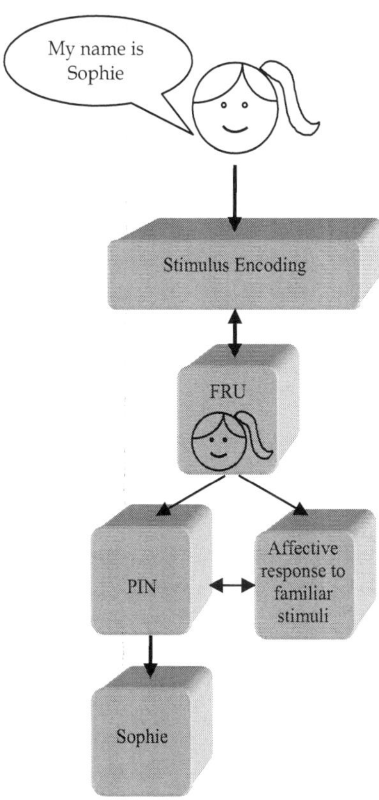

Fig. 2. A simplified version of Breen's serial model based on Bauer's theory. Two independent cognitive pathways leading to the person's identification but one anatomical route (Breen et al., 2000).

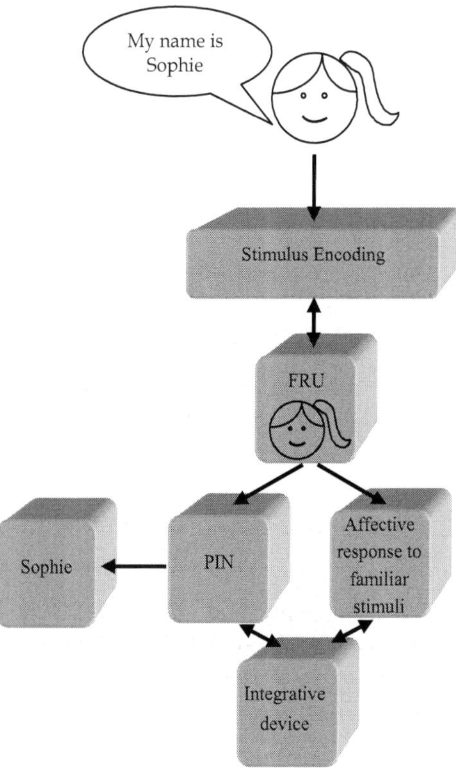

Fig. 3. An adapted version of the Ellis and Lewis model model. The Personal Identity Node (PIN) and the affective response module are connected by an integrative device (Ellis & Lewis, 2001, as cited in Henriet, 2003).

3.2.4 Ellis and Lewis add a step to Breen's model

They suggest that the information coming from the recognition system and the affective response system are re-integrated to be matched with the memorized face (Ellis & Lewis, 2001, as cited in Henriet, 2003). This processing would take place in an "integrative device". Capgras delusion would appear if the face is recognized but the familiarity response is not confirmed.

3.3 Neuro-lesional models

Neuro-lesional models of Capgras delusion were developed after cases of Capgras delusion associated with organic diseases and not just psychiatric conditions were described, for instance with migraine or cerebral localization of human immunodeficiency virus. New paraclinical tests have also become available, especially neuro-imaging techniques.

Cases of prosopagnosia have been widely studied to understand the anatomical support of face recognition. Results have been extrapolated to account for Capgras delusion.

3.3.1 A right hemisphere dysfunction

Ellis in 1994 suggested that Capgras delusion results from a right hemisphere dysfunction based on two arguments (Ellis, 1994, as cited in Henriet, 2003).

The first argument was that schizophrenia is due to a right hemisphere dysfunction (Cutting, 1985, as cited in Henriet, 2003), a hypothesis that is currently widely criticized.

The second argument was based on a literature review (Feinberg & Shapiro, 1989, as cited in Henriet, 2003) which demonstrated that the majority of patients with Capgras delusion associated with brain abnormalities (they listed 26 patients in this situation in the literature) had bilateral lesions. If lesions were unilateral (the case for 8 among the 26 patients), the lesions were most often in the right hemisphere.

His hypothesis was supported by cognitive neuropsychological data from his 1993 study where he presented two images of faces in the right or the left visual hemi-field to a group of 3 patients with Capgras delusion and to a control group of 3 patients diagnosed with schizophrenia (Ellis et al., 1993, as cited in Henriet et al., 2008). The subjects had to determine whether the two faces were identical or different, and their answer was timed. He postulated that "normal" subjects would react faster when the images are presented in the left side of their visual field, because the right cerebral hemisphere would process the stimulus faster than the left one. The results in the Capgras delusion group showed no difference between the two hemi-fields, whereas the answer was faster in the left hemi-field for the schizophrenia group. Ellis's conclusion, aside from contradicting Cutting's theory about schizophrenia, was that the face processing deficit in Capgras delusion is located in the right hemisphere.

3.3.2 Gobbini and Haxby incorporate neuro-imaging data within neuropsychological models (Gobbini & Haxby, 2007)

Recently, functional magnetic resonance imaging (fMRI) studies have found anatomic regions giving rise to face-related activity in the right hemisphere. An association of two cortical networks, a core and an extended one, are believed to be in charge of the different functions implicated in face recognition.

The core system could be composed of separate anatomical regions, like the lateral portion of the mid-fusiform gyrus or "fusiform face area" or FFA which has been discovered bilaterally but predominantly in the right hemisphere (Kanwisher et al., 1997, as cited in Gobbini & Haxby, 2007). Other occipito-temporal areas are supposed to be part of this network, such as regions in the inferior occipital gyrus (or occipital face area or OFA) or the superior temporal sulcus (or STS) (Haxby et al., 2000, as cited in Gobbini & Haxby, 2007).

This core face processing network could be further connected to an extended network for which the anatomical substrate has not been yet completely discovered, contrary to the core system.

Using Breen's neuropsychology model, the authors assume that the core system is responsible for the perception stage of face processing and the extended network for the memory operations of facial processing. The PINs are believed to be located in this extended network.

Given the anatomical segregation of these processes, damage can either appear in the specific regions or in their connections, and create various symptoms depending on where they occur. This hypothesis could support the fact that diverse lesions can lead to similar deficits, explaining the multiplicity of lesions found in neurologic Capgras delusion.

3.3.3 "Right brain lesions and left brain delusions"

Hirstein & Ramachandran in 1997, then Devinsky in 2009 postulate that Capgras delusion (and misidentification syndromes in general), when associated with a neurologic disease, is due to frontal lobes and/or right hemisphere dysfunction while specific (but unknown) left brain areas are preserved.

Right hemisphere lesions would be responsible for errors in emotions related to face stimuli and self-monitoring. Left preserved areas then "unleash a creative narrator" from these erroneous data and, since the cognitive method of classification of the left hemisphere is often binary, the patient with Capgras delusion imagines two different people instead of one.

3.3.4 Conclusion about neuro-lesional models in Capgras delusion

The paraclinical data are scarce and Capgras delusion rarely diagnosed. The explanatory models are mainly based upon prosopagnosics or neurologic Capgras. Hence it seems difficult at present to formally conclude that an anatomical lesion alone is responsible for Capgras delusion.

In addition, these theories cannot account for cases of Capgras delusion associated with psychiatric diseases where no cerebral abnormality is found, and certainly not for the case of isolated Capgras delusion described above.

The Gobbini and Haxby's model integrates paraclinical observations in neuropsychological models, opening the path to other propositions of global theories for Capgras delusion.

3.4 Global approach to Capgras delusion

The model of Capgras delusion based on Bauer's two-route theory seems confirmed by anatomical data and by neuropsychological explanations, supporting global hypotheses for the development of Capgras delusion.

Henriet in 2003 has proposed a global model integrating psychodynamic, organic and functional theories.

The first step in the development of Capgras delusion would be a functional neuropsychological deficit sometimes but not always due to organic lesions.

The patient would need to have a specific personality with "paranoid" traits and defense mechanisms such as projection or interpretation where this functional deficit would appear. All these phenomena lead to a secondary delusional rationalization, producing the symptoms of Capgras delusion.

4. Conclusion

The cleavage between organic and functional etiology is currently outdated and denied. Capgras delusion seems to be a transnosographic entity, which starts as a lesional or functional impairment, and then manifests as a psychiatric disorder.

Research in this area shows that cerebral face recognition processing is complex and not currently fully understood. Face recognition depends on a combination of anatomical structures, cognitive functions and psychopathological processing. Global approaches must be used to explore its dysfunction and function.

It is important to emphasize that, beside its scientific interest this syndrome remains a real source of pain for patients and their caretakers.

5. References

American Psychiatric Association (2000). *Diagnostic and Statistical Manual of Mental Disorders, Fourth Edition – Text Revision (DSM IV-TR)*. APA, Washington

Breen, N.; Caine, D. & Coltheart M. (2000). Models of face recognition and delusional misidentification: a critical review. Cog neuropsychol, 17, 55-71

Bruyer, R. & Scweich M. (1991). A clinical test battery of face processing. Intern. J. Neuroscience, 61, 19-30

Capgras, J. & Reboul-Lachaux, J. (1923). L'illusion des "sosies" dans un délire systématisé chronique. *Bul Soc Clin Med Ment*, 11, 6-16

Courbon, P. & Tusques, J. (1932). Illusions d'intermétamorphose et de charme. *Ann Med Psychol*, 90, 401-405

Devinsky, O. (2009). Neurology, 72, 80-87

Gobbini, M.I. & Haxby, J. (2007). Neural systems for recognition of familiar faces. Neuropsychologia, 45, 32-41

Ellis, H.D. (2004). Cognitive neuropsychology and delusional misidentification of persons. *Ann Med Psychol*, 162, 50-54

Henriet, K. (2003). *L'illusion des sosies de Capgras : syndrome ou symptôme ? Revue de la littérature*, thèse pour le doctorat en médecine, faculté de Rouen

Henriet, K. ; Haouzir, S. & Petit, M. (2008). L'illusion des sosies de Capgras : une interprétation délirante d'un trouble spécifique de la reconnaissance des visages. Revue de la littérature et proposition d'un modèle séquentiel. *Ann Med Psychol*, 166, 147-156

Hirstein, W. & Ramachandran, V. S. (1997). Capgras syndrome: a novel probe for understanding the neural representation of the identity and familiarity of persons. Proc Soc Lond, 264, 437-444

Luauté, J.P. (2009). Neuropsychiatrie cognitive des délires d'identification des personnes. Une revue historico-critique. *L'évolution psychiatrique*, 74, 93-121

Vanier, M. (1991). *Test de reconnaissance des visages de Benton,*

Vié, J. (1930). Un trouble de l'identification des personnes, l'illusion des sosies. *Ann Med Psychol*, 88, 214-237

Walther, S.; Federspiel, A.; Horn, H.; Wirth, M.; Bianchi, P.; Strik, W.; Müller, T. (2010). *Performance during Face Processing Differentiates Schizophrenia Patients with Delusional Misidentifications.* Psychopathology, 43, 127-136

World Health Organization (2010). *International Classification of Diseases, Tenth Revision, Clinical Modification (ICD-10-CM).* WHO, Geneva

11

Heritability of Face Recognition

Ingo Kennerknecht[1], Claudia Kischka[1], Claudia Stemper[1],
Tobias Elze[2] and Rainer Stollhoff[3]

[1]Institute of Human Genetics, Westfälische Wilhelms Universität Münster
[2]Schepens Eye Research Institute, Harvard Medical School, Boston, MA.
[3]Max Planck Institute for Mathematics in the Sciences, Leipzig
[1,3]Germany
[2]USA

1. Introduction

To access facial information about identity certainly belongs to the highest visual skills and is part of "visual intelligence" (Hoffman 1998). Faces *per se* are crucial for nonverbal communication and necessary for directing ones attention (e.g. by gaze direction) and for effective social interactions. Face perception provides a multitude of different information and awareness of that provides critical information about social status, health status, physical attractiveness, gender, age, allowing considerations about one´s, life style, nutritional condition, or eventually premature aging. Sexual attractiveness is perceived not only consciously but also unconsciously. An elevated but still physiological level of testosterone in males results in a receding forehead/hairline and is significantly more common in politicians representing "alpha leader". Woman mate preferences differ according to their cycle-based fertility status regarding among other cues men´s facial masculinity (Gangestad et al. 2010). Also, faces allow on-the-spot diagnosis of many genetic syndromes (Gorlin et al. 2001).

Face perception (to see a face as a face) is predominantly triggered by the T-shape order of eyes, nose, mouth (Tsao and Livingstone 2004). Face perception is followed by face processing which finally may result in face recognition. Humans are extremely competent to recognize someone by the face alone. This high cognitive skill is very robust and also very rapid and allows individualizing a face out of thousands of familiar and unfamiliar faces. The false-negative and false-positive rates of these multiple daily decisions appear to be extremely low. Face perception is characterized by its simultaneous sensitivity and insensitivity to subtle changes. On the one hand subtle changes complicate the representation of invariant aspects of faces necessary for face recognition. On the other hand these changeable aspects play a central role for social communication (Haxby et al. 2002). Constitution will fluctuate depending on changing life style or physical exercise which is reflected in the face like facial rash; facial skin might be clean, bright, youthful; lips might be dry, cracked, puffy; eyes might be dark, bruised appearance below the eyes. However, face recognition ability is not significantly hampered by these changes.

In principal, studies of familial segregation of variable face recognition might help to address this topic. As prosopagnosia is of increasing scientific interest it is not surprising that intra familial variability of face recognition was described recently (Schmalzl et al. 2008, Kischka 2011) (Fig. 6).

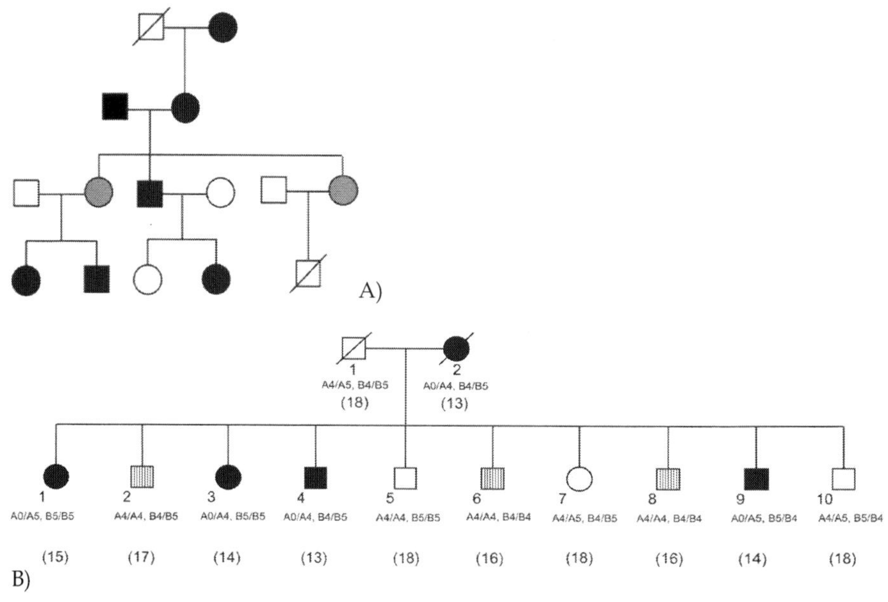

Fig. 6. Intrafamilial variability of face recognition. A) White symbols denote not impaired; black symbols denote impaired on familiarity tasks; grey symbols denote normal on familiarity task, impaired on more subtle measures of face processing (Schmalzl et al., 2008). B) White symbols denote unimpaired; shaded symbols denote face recognition ability below average; black symbols denote prosopagnosia (Kischka 2011).

Further studies will show whether the phenotypic variability follows a continuum described by a bimodal distribution (Fig. 7A) or simply by a Gaussian distribution (Fig. 7B). At the low end there are 2.5% prosopagnosics and it is assumed that at the high end there are the same number of super recognizers (Russell et al. 2009). So far this seems highly suggestive of a regular bell-shaped distribution.

2.4.5 Genetic considerations

Human face recognition is highly heritable however it´s genetic basis is unclear. Based on literature and own data an attempt is made for the genetic dissection of this higher level perception and cognition skill. Different genetic traits support one or the other finding and there is ample evidence that the complex neuronal processing also has a complex genetic background. More than 2,000 genes are involved in eye development only (Halder et al. 1995). A screening for genes that wire the (visual) cortex has been started in the mouse (review Lokmane and Garel 2011). One such approach is to look in transgenic mice for defects during embryogenesis and the functional consequences on the developing cerebral cortex. These genetic studies allow conclusions on the etiology of cerebral disorders in mice and also in humans and help to dissect the molecular pathways responsible for normal brain development.

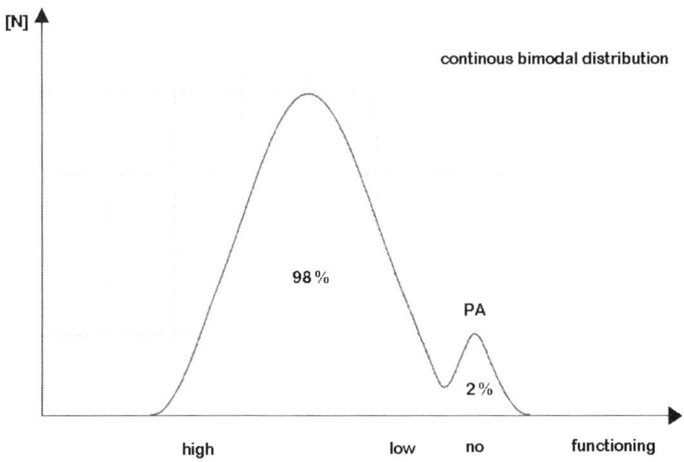

A)

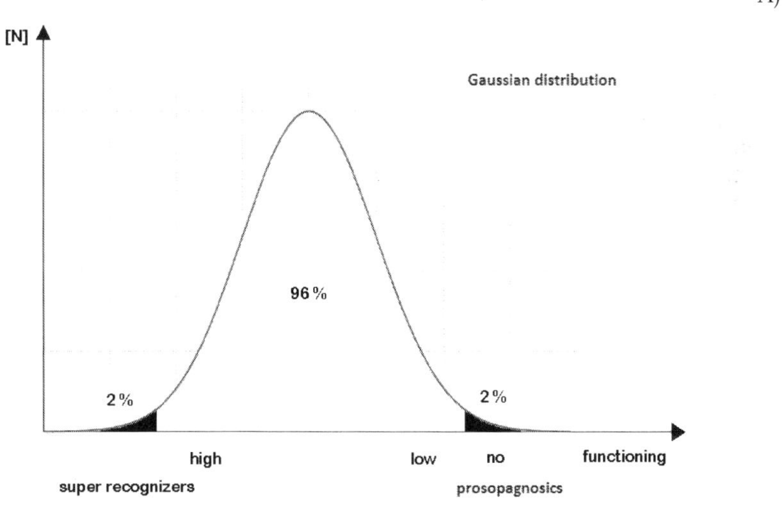

B)

Fig. 7. Face recognition ability might be continuously distributed either in a (A) bimodal way with respect to non-functioning face recognizing (prosopagnosia) or (B) alternatively, low and high performers are just tail-enders of a normal distribution.

a.   Mendelian inheritance

Already the first published cases of congenital prosopagnosia showed familiar segregation and are fully compatible with a monogenic disorder of dominant phenotypic expression (Fig. 3). Dominant in that case means that the phenotype is already expressed in the heterozygous status i.e. when only one of the two inherited parental copies (alleles) shows the mutation. This is surprising as behavioral phenotypes are part of complex genetic mechanisms, environmental influences and epigenetic modifications. One explanation might be that already one dominant acting gene mutation in the molecular cascade for the processing of face recognition interrupts or disturbs the resulting neurocognitive function. Along with such an assumption all our observations of familiar cases perfectly fit. We have meanwhile more than 100 families with recurrent prosopagnosia in two to four generations (the first 38 families of them are reported in Kennerknecht et al. 2008b). In favor of an autosomal dominant inheritance are (1) vertical transmission of the disorder, (2) males and females are equally impaired, and (3) father-to son transmission. As the father only transmits the Y-chromosome to a son (but an X-chromosome to the daughter) X-linked inheritance is excluded (Fig. 8).

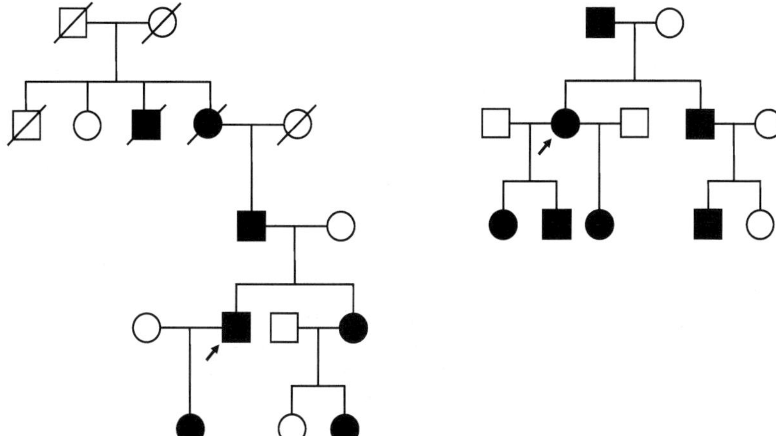

Fig. 8. Regular transmission of prosopagnosia fully compatible with autosomal dominant inheritance (modified from Grüter et al. 2007, Kennerknecht et al. 2008b)

Among 38 pedigrees (Kennerknecht et al. 2008b) only 6 exceptions were observed which are still compatible with the concept of autosomal dominant inheritance. In four families one generation is "skipped", i.e. an obligate carrier does not manifest prosopagnosia (normal transmitter) but one parent and the child(s). In two other families there is evidence of a *de novo* mutation as only one family member is impaired. It can be argued that already mutations in only one gene of the gene cascade or gene network might be sufficient in disrupting the processing of face recognition. This does not necessarily mean that all obligate carriers of such a mutation must manifest prosopagnosia. "Generation skipping" is a common phenomenon in autosomal dominant traits and is described by incomplete penetrance. Yet, it cannot be differentiated whether these are sporadic cases or isolated familial cases which are the only carriers of the mutation in a family. The genetic background (which is similar but not identical in a family) and putative epigenetic mechanisms might modify gene expression (Fig. 9). Such formal genetic considerations are extremely helpful in dissecting moleculargenetic etiology of face recognition.

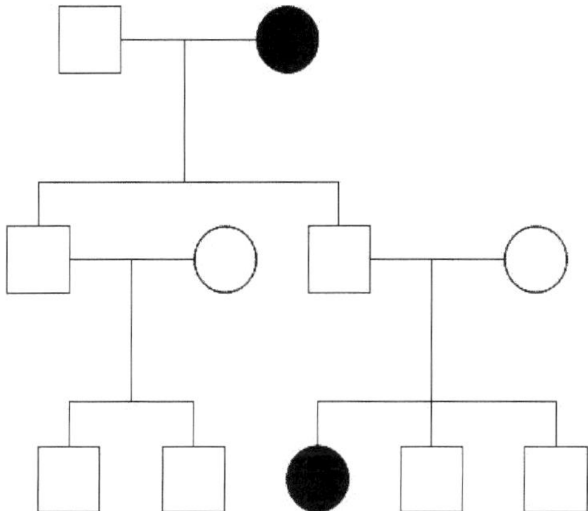

Fig. 9. Pedigree with reduced penetrance still suggestive of autosomal dominant inheritance. The father of the prosopagnosic female in the third generation is obviously a normal transmitter.

b.   Polygenic inheritance

Despite large families we still do not have candidate genes. The most plausible answer is that in a certain number of families more than one gene should be mutated (polygenic inheritance). The phenotypic variability shown in our family (Fig. 3) can be simulated in the most simple way by two genes (e.g. A and B), multiple alleles, and threshold effects at which a given phenotype is expressed. The genes A and B should have several alternative forms (i.e. alleles) e.g. gene A the alleles A0, A4, and A5, gene B the alleles B4 and B5. The figures 4 and 5 denote the relative contribution to the face recognition ability. The figure 0 (zero) describes a loss-of-function mutation and should be rare in the general population. The other alleles represent the wild type and are common. Thresholds are defined for different phenotypes of high, normal, low and no recognition (prosopagnosia) ability (Tab. 2)

Threshold value	Face recognition ability	
	Genotype	Phenotype
≥ 19	(A5/A4, B5/B5); (A5/A5, B5/B4)	Super recognizer
≥ 18	(A5/A4, B5/B4); (A4/A4, B5/B5); (A5/A5, B4/B4)	Average
≥ 16	(A5/A4, B4/B4); (A4/A4, B5/B4); (A4/A4, B4/B4);	Below average
≤ 15	(A5/**A0**, B5/B4); (A4/**A0**, B5/B5); (A5/**A0**, B5/B5); (A5/**A0**, B4/B4); (A4/**A0**, B5/B4); (A4/**A0**, B4/B4)	Prosopagnosia

Table 2. Schematic genotype-phenotype correlation of assumed digenic (genes A and B), multiallelic inheritance of face recognition. The higher the figure the more it contributes to the phenotype.

According to these assumptions the prosopagnosic mother might have the genotype A0/A4 and B4/B5 and the normal father A4/A5 and B4/B5. In a two-factor-cross of the uncoupled genes the filial generation (F1 generation) predicts a variety of genotypes and resulting phenotypes (Tab. 3).

		Paternal gametes			
		A4/B4	A4/B5	A5/B4	A5/B5
Maternal gametes	A0/B4	A0/A4, B4/B4 (12)*	A0/A4, B4/B5 (13)	A0/A5, B4/B4 (13)	A0/A5, B4/B5 (14)
	A0/B5	A0/A4, B5/B4 (13)	A0/A4, B5/B5 (14)	A0/A5, B5/B4 (14)	A0/A5, B5/B5 (15)
	A4/B4	A4/A4, B4/B4 (16)	A4/A4, B4/B5 (17)	A4/A5, B4/B4 (17)	A4/A5, B4/B5 (18)
	A4/B5	A4/A4, B5/B4 (17)	A4/A4, B5/B5 (18)	A4/A5, B5/B4 (18)	A4/A5, B5/B5 (19)

* Figures denote the relative contribution of the genotype to the phenotype of the face recognition ability.

Table 3. Genotypic and phenotypic segregation ratios of a two-factor-crossing.

According to the resulting genotypes in the filial generation (see Tab. 3) the genotypes of the family members with variable face recognition ability (see Fig. 3) are simulated (Fig. 10).

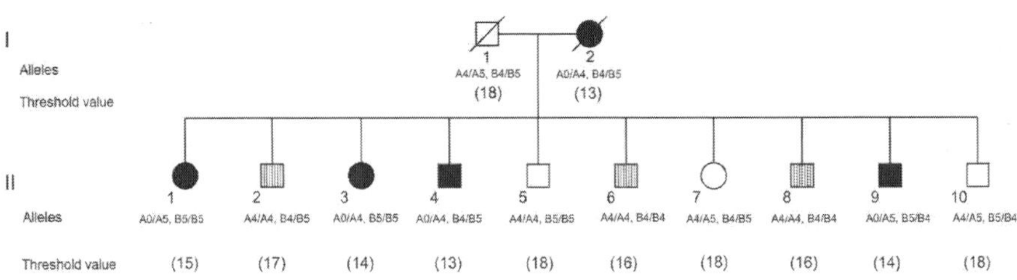

Fig. 10. Observed phenotypic distribution in a large family with assumed genotypes as derived from a hypothetic two-factor-cross (see Tab. 3).

The observed segregation ratio comes close to the expected segregation ratio (**Tab. 4**).

Face recognition ability	Expected segregation [N]	Observed segregation in the family of Fig. 7 [N]
□ / ○ average	4 (25 %)	3 (30 %)
▥ / ▦ below average	4 (25 %)	3 (30 %)
■ / ● prosopagnosia	8 (50 %)	4 (40 %)

Table 4. Genotypic and phenotypic segregation ratios of a two-factor-cross of the family described in Fig. 10.

c.   Multifactorial inheritance

In a multifactorial mode of inheritance a phenotype is not entirely defined by one or more gene(s) (i.e. monogenic or polygenic) but also significantly influenced by environment and/or experience. In short, endogenic and exogenic contribution is necessary. Twin studies are an ideal approach to evaluate the relative contribution of nature and nurture. In monocygotic twins who almost completely share the same genetic background a high concordance or discordance of a given phenotype stands for a high or low genetic influence and vice versa for a low or high environmental influence. So far twin studies show a significant genetic influence on functional brain organization as documented by functional brain imaging studies (Polk et al. 2007) and by face recognition memory tests (Willmer et al. 2010).

3. Conclusion

Face recognition ability is a high level perception and recognition skill. It remains unclear whether it is neurologically processed in a modular or in a distributed manner in the cortex or subcortical structures. Also an open question is whether face recognition ability differs from object recognition or whether it is just the top functioning end of visual recognition. At all levels a consistent finding however, is the high heritability of face recognition. So far there is no gene cloned which functions in the cascade of the visual cortex. Yet, the genetics of cerebral visual function has been shown by different approaches. Here we argue that prosopagnosia may open a window on the physiology and genetics of normal face recognition (= visual intelligence). From a large collection of prosopagnosic families phenotypic heterogeneity is obvious. Preliminary molecular genetic data also indicate genetic heterogeneity. This might be due to altered gene expression of one or more genes of the gene network associated with brain development. Depending on the impairment different familiar segregation patterns are expected either following classical modes of inheritance (Mendelian phenotype), polygenic or multifactorial inheritance and/or epigenetic modifications (Fig. 11).

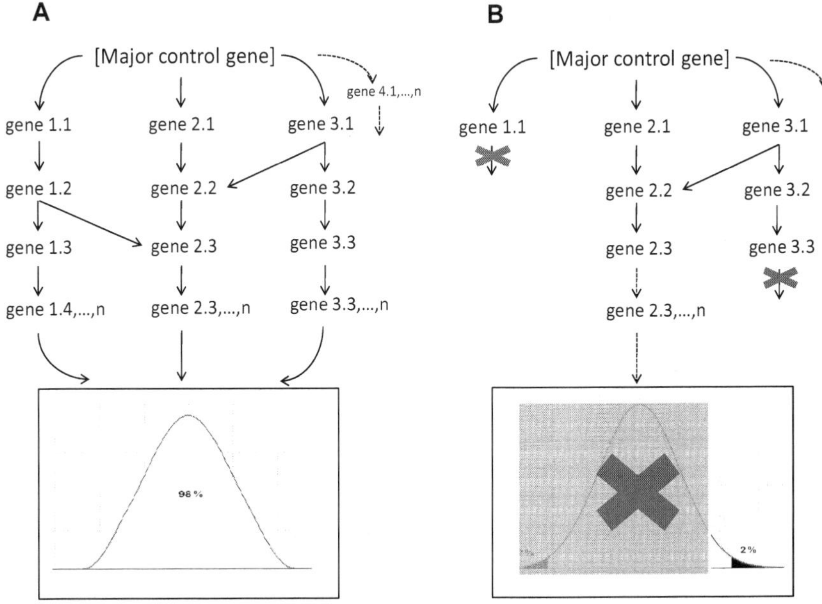

Fig. 11. A hypothetical network of genes and their respective expression that contributes to face recognition ability. Exogenic/environmental and epigenetic influences are not shown but should also play a role. A) Suggested allelic variance of the respective genes will differentially attribute to the phenotype. In a given population the face recognition ability might describe a Gaussian distribution. B) In a small subgroup one or more allelic drop-outs (e.g. by loss-of-function mutations) might occur which then result in the phenotype of poor recognizers or prosopagnosics.

By means of a permanent functional contact it can be considered that eye and brain development are simultaneously driven forward by evolution (co-evolution) as well as backward (retrograde evolution). During this process a plethora of genes had entered the network by gene duplications and successive evolutionary adaption of the duplex to its new task (intercalary evolution).

4. Acknowledgment

This project is supported by the University of Münster, Germany and approved by the local ethical committee (protocol No 3XKenn2).

5. References

Baare, W. F. C., H. E. H. Pol, D. I. Boomsma, D. Posthuma, E. J. C. de Geus, H. G. Schnack, N. E. M. van Haren, C. J. van Oel, and R. S. Kahn. "Quantitative Genetic Modeling of Variation in Human Brain Morphology." *Cerebral Cortex* 11, no. 9 (SEP, 2001): 816-824.

Behrmann, M. and G. Avidan. "Congenital Prosopagnosia: Face-Blind from Birth." *Trends in Cognitive Sciences* 9, no. 4 (APR, 2005): 180-187.

Behrmann, Marlene, Galia Avidan, Fuqiang Gao, and Sandra Black. "Structural Imaging Reveals Anatomical Alterations in Inferotemporal Cortex in Congenital Prosopagnosia." *Cerebral Cortex* 17, no. 10 (OCT, 2007): 2354-2363.

Belin, P., S. Fecteau, and C. Bedard. "Thinking the Voice: Neural Correlates of Voice Perception." *Trends in Cognitive Sciences* 8, no. 3 (MAR, 2004): 129-135.

Bodamer J. 1947. Die Prosop-Agnosie. Arch Psychiatr Nervenkr 179:6-53.

Bowles, Devin C., Elinor McKone, Amy Dawel, Bradley Duchaine, Romina Palermo, Laura Schmalzl, Davide Rivolta, C. Ellie Wilson, and Galit Yovel. "Diagnosing Prosopagnosia: Effects of Ageing, Sex, and Participant-Stimulus Ethnic Match on the Cambridge Face Memory Test and Cambridge Face Perception Test." *Cognitive Neuropsychology* 26, no. 5 (2009): 423-455.

Bruce, V. and A. Young. "Understanding Face Recognition." *British Journal of Psychology* 77, (AUG, 1986): 305-327.

Chartrand, Jean-Pierre, Isabelle Peretz, and Pascal Belin. "Auditory Recognition Expertise and Domain Specificity." *Brain Research* 1220, (JUL 18, 2008): 191-198.

Chiang, Ming-Chang, Katie L. McMahon, Greig I. de Zubicaray, Nicholas G. Martin, Ian Hickie, Arthur W. Toga, Margaret J. Wright, and Paul M. Thompson. "Genetics of White Matter Development: A DTI Study of 705 Twins and their Siblings Aged 12 to 29." *NeuroImage* 54, no. 3 (FEB 1, 2011): 2308-2317.

Cohen, J. D. and F. Tong. "Neuroscience - the Face of Controversy." *Science* 293, no. 5539 (SEP 28, 2001): 2405-2407.

Crookes, Kate and Elinor McKone. "Early Maturity of Face Recognition: No Childhood Development of Holistic Processing, Novel Face Encoding, Or Face-Space." *Cognition* 111, no. 2 (MAY, 2009): 219-247.

Deffke I (2005) Untersuchung von Gesichterpriming und Lokalisation dipolarer Quellorte der Gesichterverarbeitung in Magneto- und Elektroenzephalogramm. *Doctoral Thesis* Berlin 2005.

De Haan, E. H. F. "A Familial Factor in the Development of Face Recognition Deficits." *Journal of Clinical and Experimental Neuropsychology* 21, no. 3 (JUN, 1999): 312-315.

Della Sala S, Young AW. 2003. Quagliano´s 1867 case of prosopagnosia. Cortex 39:533-400.

Dinkelacker V, Grüter M, Klaver P, Grüter T, Specht K, Weis S, Kennerknecht I, Elger CE, Fernández G. Congenital prosopagnosia: Multistage anatomical and functional deficits in face processing circuitry. J Neurol 258: 770-782.

Downing, P. E., Y. H. Jiang, M. Shuman, and N. Kanwisher. "A Cortical Area Selective for Visual Processing of the Human Body." *Science* 293, no. 5539 (SEP 28, 2001): 2470-2473.

Dyer, A. G., C. Neumeyer, and L. Chittka. "Honeybee (Apis Mellifera) Vision can Discriminate between and Recognise Images of Human Faces." *Journal of Experimental Biology* 208, no. 24 (DEC, 2005): 4709-4714.

Egger, G., G. N. Liang, A. Aparicio, and P. A. Jones. "Epigenetics in Human Disease and Prospects for Epigenetic Therapy." *Nature* 429, no. 6990 (MAY 27, 2004): 457-463.

Eimer, M. and A. Holmes. "An ERP Study on the Time Course of Emotional Face Processing." *Neuroreport* 13, no. 4 (MAR 25, 2002): 427-431.

amplitude reduction of schizophrenia during face and facial affect processing may reflect deficient processing of facial structures and facial structure encoding.

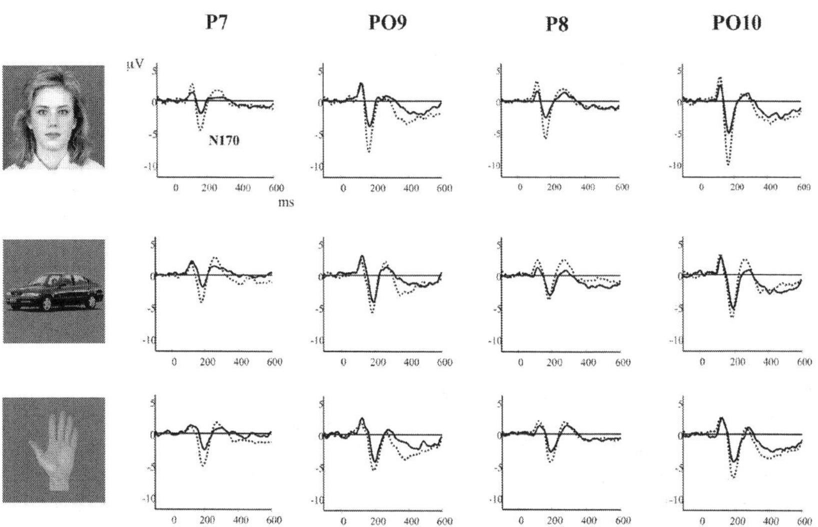

Fig. 3. The group average N170 waveforms at P7/P8 (typical N170 recording sites) and PO9/PO10 (more ventral sites with the largest effect).
The waveforms of patients with schizophrenia (n = 20) are shown in solid lines and those of normal controls (n = 16) are shown in dashed lines.

With regard to clinical correlations in patients with schizophrenia, a few studies have reported an association between the N170 and the clinical features. One study found significant associations between N170 and social dysfunction in patients with schizophrenia. Obayashi et al. (2009) reported correlations between reduced N170 amplitude in response to faces and lower Global Assessment of Functioning (GAF) scores in patients with schizophrenia. The N170 amplitude to faces could therefore function as a neurophysiological index of social functioning in schizophrenia. Further studies of social functioning of patients with schizophrenia using face processing paradigms would be of value to schizophrenia research. An fMRI study of healthy subjects suggested that the right FFA can be activated by highly trained object categories (Gauthier et al., 1999) (e.g., by birds in expert bird watchers). Moreover, Gauthier and Nelson (2001) speculate that the functional and anatomical specialization for faces in normal adults could simply be a result of our experience with human faces. As reviewed in this article, a number of findings suggest that anatomical/functional abnormalities underlie facial processing problems in patients with schizophrenia. Whether such abnormalities in schizophrenia are secondary to the limited experience of patients and/or are based on abnormalities in the neural substrate of face perception, it seems reasonable to speculate that abnormalities in face processing are related to the disinterest in social contact and social isolation observed in schizophrenic patients. In summary, a number of face-ERP studies have reported N170 amplitude reduction specific to faces, thus indicating that the neuronal populations involved in face perception may be specifically reduced in patients with schizophrenia. Moreover, schizophrenia may be characterized by deficits in the modulation of the N170 responses to different face stimuli.

10.3 N250

Beyond the N170 potential, face-sensitive potentials also exist, but only a few studies have examined the N250 potential in patients with schizophrenia. The N250 is an affect-related negative potential that occurs approximately 250 ms after the stimulus onset at fronto-central electrode sites, and is sensitive to the emotional content of a face and familiar faces (Streit et al., 1999, 2001b; Tanaka et al., 2006).

In an MEG study, Streit et al. (2001a) found decreased amplitude in the 150-250 ms potential at left inferior parietal cortex, and in the 250-350 ms potential at the left inferior prefrontal cortex. In an ERP study, Streit et al. (2001b) reported decreased ERPs at frontal sites in schizophrenia patients compared to normal controls between 180-250 ms. These studies may indicate deficits in decoding of emotional information in patients with schizophrenia beyond the N170 potential.

However, the findings of previous studies tend to be mixed with regard to the N250 in patients with schizophrenia. For instance, other researchers have suggested that these deficits are secondary flow-on effects of broader deficits in the structural encoding of faces (Johnston et al., 2005; Turetsky et al., 2007), and reported abnormally small N170 amplitudes, but normal N250 responses. This finding suggested impaired facial feature encoding but unaffected emotion decoding (Johnston et al., 2005). Further research will therefore be needed to clarify this issue.

11. Conclusion

In this chapter, we have reviewed recent research on the neural mechanisms of facial recognition. Face perception may be one of the most familiar visual stimuli and the most important stimulus with regard to social interactions. Studies in monkeys showed face-selective neurons in the monkey brain. Human research to clarify the neuronal systems of face perception were also performed in patients, including those with prosopagnosia, and contributed significant information that helped in the elucidation of the human face processing system. Two models of human face processing, the Bruce and Young model and the Haxby model have so far been proposed. In addition, Bauer's model that has two neural visual pathways (the ventral stream and the dorsal stream) account for attentional face processing. The results from the study of human face processing show that there are face perception-related regions, including the FFA, STS, OFA, aMTG, the orbitofrontal cortex and the right ventrolateral prefrontal cortex, and the amygdala.

For face recognition deficits of patients with schizophrenia, this chapter reviewed findings of behavioral, structural and functional studies. Neuropsychological findings for face processing have indicated deficits in the formation and retention of memory for face configuration information in patients with schizophrenia. Brain morphometric studies have indicated that abnormalities of the FG may be associated with the pathophysiology of schizophrenia. Neurophysiologically, schizophrenia may be characterized by deficits in modulating the N170 in response to different face stimuli.

Although the respective roles of the different brain regions involved in face processing have emerged, both neuroimaging and neurophysiology studies, including FRP studies, have positively contributed to elucidating the neural network responsible for face processing in the human brain.

12. References

Addington, J. & Addington, D. (1998). Facial affect recognition and information processing in schizophrenia and bipolar disorder. *Schizophrenia Research*, Vol.32, No.3, (August 1998), pp. 171-181, ISSN 0920-9964

Adolphs, R. (2003). Cognitive Neuroscience of human social behaviour. *Nature reviews Neuroscience*, Vol.4, (2003), pp. 165-178, ISSN 1471-003X

Aguirre, GK.; Zarahn, E. & D'Esposito, M. (1998). An area within human ventral cortex sensitive to "building" stimuli. evidence and implications. *Neuron*, Vol.21, No.2, (August 1998), pp. 373-383, ISSN 0896-6273

Aleman, A. & Kahn, RS. (2005). Strange feelings. do amygdala abnormalities dysregulate the emotional brain in schizophrenia? *Progress in Neurobiology*, Vol.77, No.5, (December 2005), pp. 283-298, ISSN 0301-0082

Allison, T.; Ginter, H.; McCarthy, G.; Nobre, AC.; Puce, A.; Luby, M. & Spencer, DD. (1994). Face recognition in human extrastriate cortex. *Journal of Neurophysiology*, Vol.71, No.2, (February 1994), pp. 821-825, ISSN 0022-3077

Allison, T.; Puce, A.; Spencer, DD. & McCarthy, G. (1999). Electrophysiological studies of human face perception. I: Potentials generated in occipitotemporal cortex by face and non-face stimuli. *Cerebral Cortex*, Vol.9, No.5, (August 1999), pp. 415-430, ISSN 1047-3211

Bangalore, SS.; Goradia, DD.; Nutche, J.; Diwadkar, VA.; Prasad, KM. & Keshavan, MS. (2009). Untreated illness duration correlates with gray matter loss in first-episode psychoses. *Neuroreport*, Vol.20, No.7, (May 2009), pp. 729-734, ISSN 0959-4965

Batty, M. & Taylor, MJ. (2003). Early processing of the six basic facial emotional expressions. *Cognitive Brain Research*,Vol.17, No.3, (October 2003), pp. 613-620, ISSN 0926-6410

Bauer, RM. (1984). Autonomic recognition of names and faces in prosopagnosia. a neuropsychological application of the Guilty Knowledge Test. *Neuropsychologia*, Vol.22, No.4, (1984), pp. 457-469, ISSN 0028-3932

Bentin, S.; Allison, T.; Puce, A.; Perez, E. & McCarthy, G. (1996). Electrophysiological studies of face perception in humans. *Journal of Cognitive Neuroscience*, Vol.8, (1996), pp551-565., ISSN 0898-929X

Bentin, S. & Deouell, LY. (2000). Structural encoding and identification in face processing. ERP evidence for separate mechanisms. *Cognitive Neuropsychology*, Vol.17, No.1, (February 2000), pp. 35-54, ISSN 0264-3294

Blair, RJ.; Morris, JS.; Frith, CD.; Perrett, DI. & Dolan, RJ. (1999). Dissociable neural responses to facial expressions of sadness and anger. *Brain*, Vol.122, No.Pt5, (May 1999), pp. 883-893, ISSN 0006-8950

Bodamer, J. (1947). Die Prosop-Agnosie. *Archiv fur Psychiatrie und Nervenkrankheiten*, Vol.179, (1947), pp. 6-54, ISSN 0003-9373

Bonda, E.; Petrides, M.; Ostry, D. & Evans, A. (1996). Specific involvement of human parietal systems and the amygdala in the perception of biological motion. *The Journal of Neuroscience*.Vol.16, (1996), pp. 3737-3744, ISSN 0898-929X

Botzel, K. & Grusser, OJ. (1989). Electric brain potentials evoked by pictures of faces and non-faces. a search for "face-specific" EEG-potentials. *Experimental Brain Research.* Vol.77, (1989) pp. 349-360, ISSN 0014-4819

Botzel, K.; Schulze, S. & Stodieck, SR. (1995). Scalp topography and analysis of intracranial sources of face-evoked potentials. *Experimental Brain Research*, Vol.104, No.1, (1995), pp. 135-143, ISSN 0014-4819

Bruce, V. & Young, A. (1986). Understanding face recognition. *British Psychological Society*, Vol.77, No (Pt 3), (1986), pp. 305-327, ISSN 1359-107X

Caharel, S.; Bernard, C.; Thibaut, F.; Haouzir, S.; Di Maggio-Clozel, C,; Allio, G.; Fouldrin, G.; Petit, M., Lalonde, R. & Rebaï, M. (2007). The effects of familiarity and emotional expression on face processing examined by ERPs in patients with schizophrenia. *Schizophrenia Research,* Vol.95, No.1-3, (September 2007), pp. 186-196, ISSN 0920-9964

Calder, AJ.; Lawrence, AD.; Keane, J.; Scott, SK.; Owen, AM.; Christoffels, I. & Young, AW. (2002). Reading the mind from eye gaze. *Neuropsychologia,* Vol.40, No.,8 (August 2002), pp. 1129-1138, ISSN 0088-3932

Calvert, GA.; Bullmore, ET.; Brammer, MJ.; Campbell, R.; Williams, SC.; McGuire, PK.; Woodruff, PW.; Iversen, SD. & David, AS. (1997). Activation of auditory cortex during silent lipreading. *Science,* Vol.276, No.5312, (April 1997), pp. 593-596, ISSN 0193-4511

Campanella, S.; Montedoro, C.; Streel, E.; Berbanck, P. & Rosier, V. (2006). Early visual components (P100.; N170) are disrupted in chronic schizophrenic patients. an event-related potentials study. *Neurophysiologie Clinique,* Vol.36, No.2, (March 2006), pp. 71-78, ISSN 0987-7053

Chao, LL.; Haxby, JV. & Martin, A. (1999a). Attribute-based neural substrates in temporal cortex for perceiving and knowing about objects. *Nature Neuroscience,* Vol.10, No.2, (October 1999), pp. 913-919, ISSN 1097-6256

Chao, LL.; Martin, A. & Haxby, JV. (1999b). Are face-responsive regions selective only for faces? *Neuroreport,* Vol.29, No.10, (September 1999), pp. 2945-2950, ISSN 0959-4965

Clark, VP.; Keil, K.; Maisog, JM.; Courtney, S.; Ungerleider, LG. & Haxby, JV. (1996). Functional magnetic resonance imaging of human visual cortex during face matching. a comparison with positron emission tomography. *Neuroimage,* Vol.4, No.1, (August 1996), pp. 1-15, ISSN 1053-8119

Damasio, A.; Damasio, H. & Van Hoesen, GW. (1982). Prosopagnosia. anatomic basis and behavioral mechanisms. *Neurology,* Vol.32, No.4, (April 1982), pp. 331-341, ISSN 0028-3878

Damasio, AR.; Tranel, D. & Rizzo, M. (2000). Disorders of complex visual processing., In: *Principles of Behavioral and Cognitive Neurology,* Mesulam, MM., pp. 335-339, Oxford University Press Inc., ISBN-13: 978-0195134759, New York.

Davis, PJ. & Gibson, MG. (2000). Recognition of posed and genuine facial expressions of emotion in paranoid and nonparanoid schizophrenia. *Journal of Abnormal Psychology,* Vol.109, No.3, (August 2000), pp. 445-450, ISSN 0021-843X

Decety, J. & Grezes, J. (1999). Neural mechanisms subserving the perception of human actions. *Trends in Cognitive Sciences*, Vol., No.5, (May 1999), pp. 172-178, ISSN 1364-6613

Di Russo, F. & Spinelli, D.(1999) Electrophysiological evidence for an early attentional mechanism in visual processing in humans. (1999). *Vision Research*, Vol.39, No.18, (September 1996), pp. 2975-2985, ISSN 0042-6989

Doniger, GM.; Foxe, JJ.; Murray, MM.; Higgins, BA. & Javitt, DC. (2002). Impaired visual object recognition and dorsal/ventral stream interaction in schizophrenia. *Archives of General Psychiatry*, Vol.59, No.11, (Novemer 2002), pp. 1011-1020, ISSN 0003-990X

Edwards, J.; Jackson, HJ. & Pattison, PE. (2002). Emotion recognition via facial expression and affective prosody in schizophrenia. a methodological review. *Clinical Psychology Review*, Vol.22, No.6, (July 2002), pp. 789-832, ISSN 0272-7358

Eifuku, S.; De Souza, WC.; Tamura, R.; Nishijo, H. & Ono, T. (2004). Neuronal correlates of face identification in the monkey anterior temporal cortical areas, *Journal of Neurophysiology*, Vol.91, No.1, (January 2004), pp. 358-371, ISSN 0022-3077

Eimer, M. & Holmes, A. (2002). An ERP study on the time course of emotional face processing. *Neuroreport*, Vol.13, No.2, (January 2003), pp. 427-431, ISSN 1530-7026

Eimer, M. (2000). The face-specific N170 component reflects late stages in the structural encoding of faces. *Neuroreport*, Vol.11, (2000), pp. 2319-2324, ISSN 0959-4965

Ekman, P. & Friesen, WV. (1978). Facial Action Coding System. Palo Alto.; CA. *Consulting Psychologists Press. Inc.*

Ekman, P. (1972). Universals and cultural differences in facial expressions of emotion. *Journal of Personality and Social Psychology*, Vol.53, No.4, (October 1972), pp.712-717, ISSN 0022-3514

Ekman, P. (1994). Strong evidence for universals in facial expressions. a reply to Russell's mistaken critique. *Psychological Bulletin*, Vol.115, No.2, (March 1994), pp. 268-287, ISSN 0734-3124

Ellis, HD. & Young, AW. (1990). Accounting for delusional misidentifications. *British Psychological Society*, Vol.157, (1990), pp. 239-248, ISSN 1359-107X

Epstein, R. & Kanwisher, N. (1998). A cortical representation of the local visual environment. *Nature*, Vol.6676, No.392, (April 1998), pp. 598-601, ISSN 0028-0836

Farah, MJ. (1991). Patterns of co-occurrence among the associative agnosias. implications for visual object representation. *Cognitive Neuropsychology*, Vol.8, (1991), pp. 1-19, ISSN 0264-3294

Farroni, T.; Csibra, G.; Simion, F. & Johnonson, MH. (2002). Eye contact detection in humans from birth, *Proceedings of the National Academy of Sciences of the United States of America*, Vol.99, No.14, (July 2002), pp. 9602-9605, ISSN 0027-8424

Gaebel, W. & Wolwer, W. (1992). Facial expression and emotional face recognition in schizophrenia and depression. *European Archives of Psychiatry and Clinical Neuroscience*, Vol.242, No.1, (1992), pp. 46-52, ISSN 0940-1334

Gauthier, I. & Nelson, CA. (2001). The development of face expertise. *Current Opinion in Neurobiology*, Vol.11, No.2, (April 2001), pp. 291-224, ISSN 0959-4388

Gauthier, I. & Tarr, MJ. (1997). Becoming a "Greeble" expert. exploring mechanisms for face recognition. *Vision Research*, Vol.37, No.12, (Junuary 1997), pp. 1673-1682, ISSN. 0042-6989

Gauthier, I.; Tarr, MJ.; Anderson, AW.; Skudlarski, P. & Gore, JC. (1999). Activation of middle fusiform 'face area' increases with expertise in recognizing novel objects. *Nature Neuroscience*, Vol.6, No.2, (Junuary 1999), pp. 568-573, ISSN 1097-6256

Goffaux, V.; Gauthier, I. & Rossion, B. (2003). Spatial scale contribution to early visual differences between face and object processing. Brain Research. *Cognitive Brain Research*, Vol.16, No.3, (May 2003), pp. 416-424, ISSN 0926-6410

Goghari, VM.; Macdonald, AW 3rd. & Sponheim, SR. (in press). Temporal lobe structures and facial emotion recognition in schizophrenia patients and nonpsychotic relatives. *Schizophrenia bulletin,* (in press), ISSN 1787-9965

Gorno-Tempini, ML.; Pradelli, S.; Serafini, M.; Pagnoni, G.; Baraldi, P.; Porro, C.; Nicoletti, R.; Umità, C. & Nichelli, P. (2001). Explicit and incidental facial expression processing. an fMRI study. *Neuroimage*, Vol.14, No.2, (August 2001), pp. 465-473, ISSN 1053-8119

Green, MJ. & Phillips, ML. (2004). Social threat perception and the evolution of paranoia. *Neuroscience and Biobehavioral Reviews*, Vol.28, No3., (May 2004), pp. 333-342, ISSN. 0149-7634

Grill-Spector, K.; Knouf, N. & Kanwisher, N. (2004). The fusiform face area subserves face perception.; not generic within-category identification. *Nature Neuroscience*, Vol.7, No.5, (May 2004), pp. 555-562, ISSN 1097-6256

Grossman, E.; Donnelly, M.; Price, R.; Pickens, D.; Morgan, V.; Neighbor, G. & Blake, R. (2000). Brain areas involved in perception of biological motion. *Journal of Cognitive Neuroscience*, Vol.12, (2000), pp. 711-720, ISSN 0898-929X

Gur, RC.; Sara, R.; Hagendoorn, M.; Marom, O.; Hughett, P.; Macy, L.; Turner, T.; Bajcsy, R.; Posner, A. & Gur, RE. (2002). A method for obtaining 3-dimensional facial expressions and its standardization for use in neurocognitive studies. *Journal of Neuroscience Methods*, Vol.115, No.2, (April 2002), pp. 137-143, ISSN 0165-0270

Haenschel, C.; Bittner, RA.; Haertling, F.; Rotarska-Jagiela, A.; Maurer, K.; Singer, W. & Linden, DE. (2008). Contribution of impaired early-stage visual processing to working memory dysfunction in adolescents with schizophrenia. a study with event-related potentials and functional magnetic resonance imaging. *Archives of General Psychiatry*, Vol.64, No.11, (November 2007), pp. 1229-1240, ISSN 0003-990X

Halgren, E.; Dale, AM.; Sereno, MI.; Tootell, RB.; Marinkovic, K. & Rosen, BR. (1999). Location of human face-selective cortex with respect to retinotopic areas. *Human Brain Mapping*, Vol.7, No.1, (1999), pp. 29-37, ISSN. 1065-9471

Hasselmo, ME.; Rolls, ET. & Baylis, GC. (1989). The role of expression and identity in the face-selective responses of neurons in the temporal visual cortex of the monkey, *Behavioural Brain Research*, Vol.32, No.3, (April 1989), pp. 203-218, ISSN 0166-4328

Haxby, JV.; Hoffman, EA. & Gobbini, MI. (2002). Human neural systems for face recognition and social communication. *Biological Psychiatry*, Vol.51, No.1, (January 2002), pp. 59-67, ISSN 0006-3223

Haxby, JV.; Hoffman, EA. & Gobbini, MI. (2000). The distributed human neural system for face perception. *Trends in Cognitive Sciences*, Vol.4, (2000), pp. 223-233, ISSN 1364-6613

Haxby, JV.; Ungerleider, LG.; Clark VP.; Schouten, JL.; Hoffman, EA. & Martin, A. (1999). The effect of face inversion on activity in human neural systems for face and object perception. *Neuron*, Vol.22, No.1, (January 1999), pp. 189-199, ISSN 0896-6273

Henson, RN.; G-GY.; Ganel, T.; Otten, LJ.; Quayle, A. & Rugg, MD. (2003). Electrophysiological and haemodynamic correlates of face perception.; recognition and priming. *Cereb Cortex*, Vol.13, No.7, (July 2003), pp 793-805, ISSN 1047-3211

deficits. *Cognitive Neuropsychology*. Vol.17, No.1, (February 2000), pp. 187-199, ISSN 0264-3294

Martin, A. & Chao, LL. (2001). Semantic memory and the brain. structure and processes. *Current Opinion in Neurobiology*, Vol.11, (2001), pp. 194-201, ISSN 0959-4388

Morris, JS.; DeGelder, B.; Weiskrantz, L. & Dolan, RJ. (2001). Differential extrageniculostriate and amygdala responses to presentation of emotional faces in cortically blind field. *Brain*, Vol.124, No.Pt6, (Junuary 2001), pp. 1241-1252, ISSN 0006-8950

Morris, JS.; Friston, KJ.; Buchel, C.; Frith, CD.; Young AW.; Calder, AJ. & Dolan, RJ. (1998). A neuromodulatory role for the human amygdala in processing emotional facial expressions. *Brain*, Vol121., No.Pt1, (January 1998), pp. 47-57, ISSN 0006-8950

Morton, J. & Johnson, MH. (1991). CONSPEC and CONLERN: a two-process theory of infant face recognition, *Psychological Review*, Vol.98, No.2, (April 1991), pp. 164-181, ISSN 0033-295X

Naidich, TP.; Daniels, DL.; Haughton, VM.; Williams, A.; Pojunas, K. & Palacios, E. (1987). Hippocampal formation and related structures of the limbic lobe. anatomic-MR correlation. *Radiology*, Vol.162, No.3, (March 1987), pp. 747-754, ISSN 0033-8419

Nakamura, K.; Kawashima, R.; Sato, N.; Nakamura, A.; Sugiura, M.; Kato, T.; Hatano, K.; Ito, K.; Fukuda, H.; Schormann, T. & Zilles, K. (2000). Functional delineation of the human occipito-temporal areas related to face and scene processing. A PET study. *Brain*, Vol.123, No.Pt9, (Septenber 2000), pp. 1903-1912, ISSN 0006-8950

Nakamura, K.; Mikami, A. & Kubota, K. (1992). Activity of single neurons in the monkey amygdala during performance of a visual discrimination task, *Journal of Neurophysiology*, Vol.67, No.6, (June 1992), pp. 1447-1463, ISSN 0022-3077

Narumoto, J.; Okada, T.; Sadato, N.; Fukui, K. & Yonekura, Y. (2001). Attention to emotion modulates fMRI activity in human right superior temporal sulcus. *Cognitive Brain Research*, Vol.12, No.2, (October 2001), pp. 225-231, ISSN 0926-6410

Obayashi, C.; Nakashima, T.; Onitsuka, T.; Maekawa, T.; Hirano, Y.; Hirano, S.; Oribe, N.; Kaneko, K.; Kanba, S. & Tobimatsu, S. (2009). Decreased spatial frequency sensitivities for processing faces in male patients with chronic schizophrenia. *Clinical Neurophysiology*, Vol.120, No.8, (August 2009), pp. 1525-1533, ISSN 1388-2457

Onitsuka, T.; Nestor, PG.; Gurrera, RJ.; Shenton, ME.; Kasai, K.; Frumin, M.; Niznikiewicz, MA. & McCarley, RW. (2005). Association between reduced extraversion and right posterior fusiform gyrus gray matter reduction in chronic schizophrenia. *The American Journal of Psychiatry*, Vol.162, No.3, (March 2005), pp. 599-601, ISSN 0002-953X

Onitsuka, T.; Niznikiewicz, MA.; Spencer, KM.; Frumin, M.; Kuroki, N.; Lucia, LC.; Shenton, ME. & McCarley, RW. (2006). Functional and structural deficits in brain regions subserving face perception in schizophrenia. *The American Journal of Psychiatry*, Vol.163, No.3, (March 2006), pp. 455-462, ISSN 0002-953X

Onitsuka, T.; Shenton, ME.; Kasai, K.; Nestor, PG.; Toner, SK.; Kikinis, R.; Jolesz, FA. & McCarley, RW. (2003). Fusiform gyrus volume reduction and facial recognition in chronic schizophrenia. *Archives of General Psychiatry*, Vol.60, No.8, (August 2003), pp. 349-355, ISSN 0003-990X

Ono, M.; Kubik, S. & Abernathey, CD. (1990). *Atlas of the cerebral sulci*. Georg Thieme Verlag, ISBN-13: 978-0865773622, New York

Oram, MW. & Perrett, DI. (1996). Integration of form and motion in the anterior superior temporal polysensory area (STPa) of the macaque monkey, *Journal of Neurophysiology*, Vol.76, No.1, (July 1996), pp. 109-129, ISSN 0022-3077

Paille-Martinot, ML.; Caclin, A.; Artiges, E.; Poline, JB.; Joliot, M.; Mallet, L.; Recasens, C.; Attar-Lévy, D. & Martinot, JL. (2001). Cerebral gray and white matter reductions and clinical correlations in patients with early onset schizophrenia. *Schizophrenia Research*, Vol.50, No.1-2, (May 2001), pp. 19-26, ISSN 0920-9964

Perrett, DI.; Smith, PA.; Mistlin, AJ.; Chitty, AJ.; Head, AS.; Potter, DD.; Broennimann, R.; Milner, AD. & Jeeves, MA. (1985). Visual analysis of body movements by neurones in the temporal cortex of the macaque monkey. a preliminary report. *Behavioural Brain Research*, Vol.16, No.2-3, (August 1985), pp. 153-170, ISSN 0166-4328

Perrett, DI.; Smith, PA.; Potter, DD.; Mistlin, AJ.; Head, AS.; Milner, AD. & Jeeves, MA. (1984). Neurones responsive to faces in the temporal cortex. studies of functional organization, sensitivity to identity and relation to perception, *Human Neurobiology*, Vol.4, No.3, (1984), pp. 197-208, ISSN 0721-9075

Phillips, ML.; Williams, L.; Senior, C.; Bullmore, ET.; Brammer, MJ.; Andrew, C.; Williams, SCR. & David, AS. (1999). A differential neural response to threatening and non-threatening negative facial expressions in paranoid and non-paranoid schizophrenics. *Psychiatry Research*, Vol.92, No.1, (November 1999), pp. 11-31, ISSN 0165-1781

Pourtois, G.; Dan, ES.; Grandjean, D.; Sander, D. & Vuilleumier, P. (2005). Enhanced extrastriae visual response to bandpass spatial frequency filtered fearful faces. time course and topographic evoked-potentials mapping. *Human Brain Mapping*,Vol26., No.1, (September 2005), pp. 65-79, ISSN 1065-9471

Premkumar, P.; Fannon, D.; Kuipers, E.; Cooke, MA.; Simmons, A. & Kumari, V. (2008). Association between a longer duration of illness, age and lower frontal lobe grey matter volume in schizophrenia. *Behavioural Brain Research*, Vol.193, No.1, (November 2008), pp. 132-139, ISSN 0166-4328

Puce, A.; Allison, T.; Bentin, S.; Gore, JC. & McCarthy, G. (1998). Temporal cortex activation in humans viewing eye and mouth movements. *The Journal of Neuroscience*, Vol.18, No.6, (March 1998), pp. 2188-2199, ISSN 0976-3155

Puce, A.; Epling, JA.; Thompson, JC. & Carrick, OK. (2007). Neural responses elicited to face motion and vocalization pairings. *Neuropsychologia*, Vol.45, No.1, (January 2007), pp. 93-106, ISSN 0028-3932

Quintana, J.; Wong, T.; Ortiz-Portillo, E.; Marder, SR. & Mazziotta, JC. (2003) Right lateral fusiform gyrus dysfunction during facial information processing in schizophrenia. *Biological Psychiatry*, Vol.53, No.12, (Junuary 2003), pp. 1099-1112, ISSN 0006-3223

Rebai, M.; Bernard, C.; Lannou, J. & Jouen, F. (1998). Spatial frequency and right hemisphere. an electrophysiological investigation. *Brain and Cognition*, Vol.36, No.1, (February 1998), pp. 21-29, ISSN 0278-2626

Rolls, ET.; Critchley, HD.; Browning, AS. & Inoue, K. (2006). Face-selective and auditory neurons in the primate orbitofrontal cortex. *Experimental Brain Research*, Vol.170, No.1, (March 2006), pp. 74-87, ISSN 0014-4819

Rossion, B.; Delvenne, JF.; Debatisse, D.; Goffaux, V.; Bruyer, R.; Crommelinck, M. & Guérit, JM. (1999). Spatio-temporal localization of the face inversion effect. an event-related potentials study. *Biological Phychology*, Vol.50, No.3, (July 1999), pp. 173-189, ISSN 0301-0511

Rossion, B.; Gauthier, I.; Goffaux, V.; Tarr, MJ. & Crommelinck, M. (2002). Expertise training with novel objects leads to left lateralized face-like electrophysiological responses. *Psychological Science*,Vol.13, No.3, (May 2002), pp. 250-257, ISSN 0956-7976

Rossion, B.; Gauthier, I.; Tarr, MJ.; Despland, P.; Bruyer, R.; Linotte, S. & Crommelinck, M. (2000). The N170 occipito-temporal component is delayed and enhanced to inverted faces but not to inverted objects. an electrophysiological account of face-specific processes in the human brain. *Neuroreport*, Vol.11, No.1, (January 2000), pp. 69-74, ISSN 0959-4965

Schechter, I.; Butler, PD.; Zemon, V.; Revheim, N.; Saperstein, AM.; Jalbrzikowski, M.; Pasternak, R.; Silipo, G. & Javitt, DC. (2005). Impairments of earlystage transient visual evoked potentials to magno- and parvocellular-selective stimuli in schizophrenia. *Clinical Neurophysiology*, Vol.116, No.9, (September 2005), pp.2204-2215, ISSN 1388-2457

Sergent, J.; Ohta, S. & MacDonald, B. (1992). Functional neuroanatomy of face and object processing. A positron emission tomography study. *Brain*, (February 1992), Pt 1. 15-36, ISSN 0006-8950

Sheline, YI.; Barch, DM.; Donnelly, JM.; Ollinger, JM.; Snyder, AZ. & Mintun, MA. (2001). Increased amygdala response to masked emotional faces in depressed subjects resolves with antidepressant treatment. an fMRI study. *Biological Psychiatry*, Vol.50, No.1, (November 2001), pp. 651-658,ISSN. 0006-3223

Shenton, ME.; Dickey, CC.; Frumin, M. & McCarley, RW. (2001). A review of MRI findings in schizophrenia. *Schizophrenia Research*, Vol.49, No.1-2, (April 2001), pp. 1-52, ISSN 0920-9964

Silver, H.; Shlomo, N.; Turner, T. & Gur, RC. (2002). Perception of happy and sad facial expressions in chronic schizophrenia. evidence for two evaluative systems. *Schizophrenia Research*, Vol.55, No.1-2, (May 2002), pp. 171-177, ISSN 0920-9964

Smith, NK.; Cacioppo, JT.; Larsen, JT. & Chartrand, TL. (2003). May I have your attention, please: electrocortical responses to positive and negative stimuli. *Neuropsychologia*, Vol.41, No.2, (2003), pp. 171-183, ISSN 0028-3932.

Spiridon, M. & Kanwisher, N. (2002). How distributed is visual category information in human occipito-temporal cortex? An fMRI study. *Neuron*, Vol.35, No.6, (September 2002), pp. 1157-1165, ISSN 0896-6273

Streit, M.; Ioannides, AA.; Sinneman, T.; Wolwer, W.; Dammers, J.; Zilles, K. & Gaebel, W. (2001a). Disturbed facial affect recognition in patients with schizophrenia associated with hypoactivity in distributed brain regions: a magnetoencephalographic study. *The American Journal of Psychiatry*, Vol.158, No.9, (September 2001), pp. 1429-1436, ISSN 0002-953X

Streit, M.; Ioannides, AA.; Liu, L.; Wolwer, W.; Dammers, J.; Gross, J.; Gaebel, W. & Müller-Gärtner, HW. (1999). Neurophysiological correlates of the recognition of facial expressions of emotion as revealed by magnetoencephalography. *Cognitive Brain Research*, Vol.7, No.1, (February 1999), pp. 481-491, ISSN 0926-6410

Streit, M.; Wolwer, W.; Brinkmeyer, J. Ihl, R. & Gaebel, W. (2001b). EEG correlates of facial affect recognition and categorisation of blurred faces in schizophrenic patients and healthy volunteers. *Schizophrenia Research*, Vol.49, No.1-2, (April 2001), pp. 145-155, ISSN 0920-9964

Surguladze, S.; Russell, T.; Kucharska-Pietura, K.; Travis, MJ.; Giampietro, V.; David, AS. & Phillips, ML. (2006). A reversal of the normal pattern of parahippocampal response to neutral and fearful faces is associated with reality distortion in schizophrenia. *Biological Psychiatry*, Vol.60, No.5, (September 2006), pp. 423-431, ISSN 0006-3223

Tanaka, JW.; Curran, T.; Porterfield, AL. & Collins, D. (2006). Activation of preexisting and acquired face representations. the N250 event-related potential as an index of face familiarity. *Journal of Cognitive Neuroscience*, Vol.18, No.9, (September 2006), pp. 1488-1497, ISSN. 0898-929X

Tanaka, JW. & Curran, T. (2001). A neural basis for expert object recognition. *Psychological Science*, Vol.12, (2001), pp. 43-47 ISSN 0956-7976

Thorpe, SJ.; Rolls, ET. & Maddison, S. (1983). The orbitofrontal cortex. neuronal activity in the behaving monkey, *Experimental Brain Research*, Vol.49, No.1, (1983), pp. 93-115, ISSN 0014-4819

Tobimatsu, S.; Kurita-Tashima, S.; Nakayama-Hiromatsu, M.; Akazawa, K. & Kato, M. (1993). Age-related changes in pattern visual evoked potentials. differential effects of luminance.; contrast and check size. *Electroencephalography and clinical Neurophysiology*, Vol.88, No.1, (January 1993), pp. 12-19, ISSN 0013-4694

Tong, F.; Nakayama, K.; Moscovitch, M.; Weinrib, O. & Kanwisher, N. (2000). Response properties of the human fusiform face area. *Cognitive Neuropsychology*,Vol.17, No.1, (February 2000), pp. 257-280, ISSN 0264-3294

Turetsky, BI.; Kohler, CG.; Indersmitten, T.; Bhati, MT.; Charbonnier, D. & Gur, RC. (2007). Facial emotion recognition in schizophrenia: when and why does it go awry? *Schizophrenia Research*, Vol.94, No.1-3, (August 2007), pp. 253-263, ISSN 0920-9964

Vignal, JP.; Chauvel, P. & Halgren, E. (2000). Localised face processing by the human prefrontal cortex. stimulation-evoked hallucinations of faces. *Cognitive Neuropsychology*, Vol.17, No.1, (February 2000), pp. 281-291, ISSN 0264-3294

Vuilleumier, P. (2000). Faces call for attention. evidence from patients with visual extinction. *Neuropsychologia*, Vol. 38, No.5, (2000), pp. 693-700, ISSN 0028-3932

Wada, Y. & Yamamoto, T. (2001). Selective impairment of facial recognition due to a haematoma restricted to the right fusiform and lateral occipital region. *Journal of Neurology, Neurosurgery, and Psychiatry*, Vol.71, No.2, (August 2001), pp. 254-257, ISSN 0022-3050

Watanabe, S.; Kakigi, R.; Koyama, S. & Kirino E. (1999). Human face perception traced by magneto- and electro-encephalography. *Cognitive Brain Research*, Vol.8, No.2, (July 1999), pp. 125-142, ISSN 0926-6410

Wilson, FA.; Scalaidhe, SP. & Goldman-Rakic, PS. (1993). Dissociation of object and spatial processing domains in primate prefrontal cortex. *Science*, Vol.5116, No.260, (Junuary 1993), pp. 1955-1958, ISSN 0193-4511

Winston, JS.; Strange, BA.; O'Doherty, J. & Dolan, RJ. (2002). Automatic and intentional brain responses during evaluation of trustworthiness of faces. *Nature Neuroscience*, Vol.5, No.3, (March 2002), pp. 277-283, ISSN 1097-6256

Wolwer, W.; Streit, M.; Polzer, U. & Gaebel, W. (1996). Facial affect recognition in the course of schizophrenia. *European Archives of Psychiatry and Clinical Neuroscience*, Vol.246, No.3, (1996), pp165-70., ISSN 0940-1334

Wright, IC.; Rabe-Hesketh, S.; Woodruff, PW.; David, AS.; Murray, RM. & Bullmore, ET. (2000). Meta-analysis of regional brain volumes in schizophrenia. *The American Journal of Psychiatry*, Vol.157, No.1, (January 2000), pp. 16-25, ISSN 0002-953X

Yeap, S.; Kelly, SP.; Sehatpour, P.; Magno, E.; Javitt, DC.; Garavan, H; Thakore, JH. & Foxe, JJ. (2006). Early visual sensory deficits as endophenotypes for schizophrenia. high-density electrical mapping in clinically unaffected first-degree relatives. *Archives of General Psychiatry*, Vol.63, No.11, (November 2006), pp. 1180-1188, ISSN 0003-990X